“People who know him, from the early days when he was a student and competitive swimmer, to people in the art world, and his former colleagues in DP Architects, all agree that Koh Seow Chuan has been successful in life because of one signature trait: that he places teamwork above individual glory.”

Jane Ittogi
Chair, Tasek Jurong Limited,
and wife of President Tharman Shanmugaratnam

“Most young artists find it tough in the Singapore art market, especially those without a name. Seow Chuan buys their works, keeps them, so that they can continue to create. With some artists, he even gives them allowances, and tells them they can pay him later in kind. So, while he has a lot of known artists in his collection, what is not known is, he has a lot of unknown artists too.”

Melvin Poh
Art Collector

“He has built an ecosystem with people like Melvin and us, he encourages us, involves us, and influences us, and in turn we have cultivated a lot of collectors along the way. After he retired, he has been tirelessly spending time sitting with people, talking to people about art. In the two decades since he retired, he has imparted a lot of experience and knowledge. Invaluable.”

Linda Neo and **Albert Lim**
Art Collectors

"I associate Seow Chuan with future building, he ensured that DP Architects would grow from strength to strength in the future years. According to our corporate constitution, individuals are mandated to initiate the process of relinquishing their shareholdings once they reach the age of 60. By the time they reach 65, their shareholdings must be reduced to zero. This embodies the epitome of honour and selflessness. It entails relinquishing ownership of the very company one founded, thereby affording the younger generation the opportunity to steer the organisation's growth. We can count ourselves exceedingly fortunate to have a founder of Mr Koh's calibre guiding our path."

Angelene Chan
Chairman, DP Architects

"The power of storytelling is something we cannot underestimate. For instance, the story of Mr Koh mortgaging his stamps to the bank to get the firm out of a very difficult situation. These are powerful stories that stay vivid in our minds. He has countless stories from People's Park Complex, Golden Mile Complex, to the Esplanade, stories that foster the DP identity and sense of belonging because they speak of our common and collective past. When I first met Mr Koh, he was about to retire and not as active in DP. But the stories I heard made him relevant. These are stories I will share with the next generation."

Seah Chee Huang
CEO, DP Architects

"For a high-profile person, he is unassuming, very in touch with the ground. Very accessible."

Chin Thoe Chong
Director, DP Architects

"Mr Koh Seow Chuan truly does not ask for anything in return, doesn't make you feel bad if you don't reciprocate. He gives, that's all. That's such a simple thing, yes simple but very hard to find these days. For a lot of people, they give you something, but you know they would ask you for something in return later. But not Mr Koh, he gives and tells me this is for Singapore. He always reminds me that whatever I am doing, it's for Singapore. It's not for him. Generous. And very curious. His mind is always curious. I really admire that. I am in my 30s, he is in his 80s, yet we are working so well together. Just incredible."

Dr Diana Tay
PhD in Art Conservation,
Conservation Consultant

Published by

World Scientific Publishing Co. Pte. Ltd.
5 Toh Tuck Link, Singapore 596224
USA office: 27 Warren Street, Suite 401-402, Hackensack, NJ 07601
UK office: 57 Shelton Street, Covent Garden, London WC2H 9HE

British Library Cataloguing-in-Publication Data
A catalogue record for this book is available from the British Library.

AN UNFINISHED CANVAS
Life of Koh Seow Chuan

ISBN 978-981-12-8697-1 (hardcover)
ISBN 978-981-12-8731-2 (paperback)
ISBN 978-981-12-8698-8 (ebook for institutions)
ISBN 978-981-12-8699-5 (ebook for individuals)

For any available supplementary material, please visit
https://www.worldscientific.com/worldscibooks/10.1142/13696#t=suppl

Desk Editors: Nicole Ong/Claire Lum
Design and layout: Jimmy Low

Printed in Singapore

AN UNFINISHED CANVAS

Life of Koh Seow Chuan

AN UNFINISHED CANVAS

Life of Koh Seow Chuan

Woon Tai Ho

NEW JERSEY • LONDON • SINGAPORE • BEIJING • SHANGHAI • HONG KONG • TAIPEI • CHENNAI • TOKYO

Contents

Foreword

The life and work of Koh Seow Chuan, pioneer architect, stamp collector and art patron, is a remarkable journey that transcends the realm of art and architecture. His story speaks of a commitment to innovation, creativity, and a deep desire to push boundaries and reïmagine the ordinary.

An Unfinished Canvas takes us through early milestone projects by Design Partnership and later DP Architects, co-founded by Seow Chuan, in a career mirroring Singapore's nation-building journey. From People's Park Complex to Golden Mile Complex to Esplanade — Theatres on the Bay, the most architecturally distinctive cultural edifice in Singapore, we gain glimpses of a visionary mind, his ethos to life, work and relationships shaped by a lifelong quest for knowledge and a firm belief in the power of teamwork. It was Seow Chuan with his far-sighted ideas and quiet conviction to rejuvenate the dilapidated Golden Mile Complex through creative conservation who prompted me to look deeper into the collective sale opportunity. With my joint-venture partners, we have embarked on the revitalisation of this architectural icon of post-independence Singapore with DP Architects' fourth-generation team fostered by Seow Chuan himself.

I first met Seow Chuan through Chan Sui Him, his close friend and partner at DP Architects, when they were my architects for The Bayshore on Upper East Coast Road. It was a prized government land sales site that gave Far East Organization a challenge to deliver a unique quality, high-rise, high-density living environment in a condominium which was the largest of its time in Singapore with 1,038 apartment units. Seow Chuan and his team responded to this brief from design inception through the development execution with many innovations, resulting in a product that was well ahead of its time in architectural design, construction methods, quality standards and lifestyle experience. The Bayshore achieved awards from the Construction Industry Development Board (CIDB, the predecessor of the Building and Construction Authority, BCA) for Best Buildable Design 1997 and Construction Excellence 1999, marking the first time that Far East Organization would receive the prestigious national awards.

This was the start of a deep and enduring partnership through more than three decades with project after project, many of which went on to win international acclaim, such as Far East Square, The Fullerton Heritage precinct, The Central, Novena Lifestyle and Medical Hub, Orchard Central, and Woods Square. I asked DP Architects to project manage the conservation of The Fullerton Hotel and invited Seow Chuan to be our art consultant. He did such a marvellous job curating the unique artworks which still energise the ambience decades on.

Through the chronicles of Seow Chuan's life journey, we begin to appreciate that our work is not only about building spaces but creating lifelong experiences and shared memories, that our buildings are not just physical structures, but reflections of our culture, identity, and aspirations.

Seow Chuan is a man of many varied interests and pursuits with a heart of such warmth and kindness. I recall with fondness our serendipitous meeting as members of a Singapore trade mission to South Africa in the mid-1990s. Over wine and barbecue in the picturesque vineyard he co-owns in the famous Paarl/Stellenbosch wine region, I got to know Seow Chuan better as a purveyor of ideas, always with interesting perspectives on design and property development. He still co-owns the land and ongoing development there, a testament to his long-term commitment to projects that he starts.

Seow Chuan, in his inimitable unassuming manner, has pointed to Jesus in his walk of obedience with our Almighty God. Beyond blueprints and concrete structures, he has touched many lives and enriched the communities he served through his authenticity and sincerity, by the grace of God.

May the Lord our God bless the work of Seow Chuan's hands as he continues to flourish in a new season of his life.

Philip Ng
October 2023

Thank You from

Professor Tommy Koh, for your warm friendship since the days of SPUR in the mid 1960s and early 70s. You encouraged me to take on the chairmanship of the Singapore Philatelic Museum in the mid 1990s, then the chairmanship of the Singapore Art Museum and various committees leading to the chairmanship of the National Gallery Singapore. And your unfailing confidence in DP Architects for The Esplanade — Theatres on the Bay project.

Melvin Poh, for nudging me all these years, to have a book written on my life, without which, this book would never have been written. Also, as a good friend in the art collecting journey in the last 10 years.

Linda Neo and **Albert Lim**, for encouraging me to collect art beyond Cheong Soo Pieng and Lim Tze Peng, into the world of contemporary Singapore art.

Diana Ann Tay, for carrying out research work for artist Cheong Soo Pieng of my collection, and for bringing art into the realm of science. This is important, innovative and creative work.

Dick Chia and **Ida Ng** of Helutrans Art Logistics, for allotting space for my art collection all these years and making available Helutrans Artspace for exhibiting my collection.

Seow Chuan

A Special Thank You to **Philip Ng** of Far East Organisation for over 30 years of friendship, the numerous projects you commissioned DP Architects as your design and project architect. I am humbled and touched by your kind words in the foreword to this book, thank you for agreeing to write it.

Chan Sui Him, Gan Eng Oon, Francis Lee and all at DP Architects since 1981, travelling the DP Architects journey together as a team all these years and for taking DP Architects to greater heights.

Angelene Chan, Seah Chee Huang and **Chin Thoe Chong** for representing the current leadership of DP Architects in agreeing to be interviewed for this book. I am humbled and honoured by what you said.

DPian Family from 1967 to now, taking DP to greater and greater heights around the Globe.

Woon Tai Ho for spending more than 15 months with me and my wife Wen Gin, writing my life story.

The team at **World Scientific** for producing this book.

Stamp collectors at Singapore Stamp Club since 1967, Federation of Inter-Asian Philately and Federation of International Philately stamp collectors and ALL stamp collectors around the world for sharing knowledge.

Artists for bringing JOY to life. Art Institutions for supporting artists and art collectors for sharing your collection by holding public exhibition in collaboration.

Friends, family, my wife, my four lovely children and five wonderful grandchildren for giving me a lifetime of joy and inspiration.

Prologue

The idea of a book about my life has been raised by friends and colleagues, even family members, on numerous occasions — upon my retirement, on my birthdays, as well as after conquering a major obstacle. Every time the idea was raised, I would always have a reason to veto it. I was not old enough, and there was still so much more to do, I told myself.

But if something is meant to be, it will be. Last August, a friend of mine, Melvin Poh, who is an art collector, said I should seriously consider sharing with the public what I have gone through in my life, not just to record it, but as a means of sharing what I have learnt. He felt strongly that I have much to share. I thought it through, and decided, if a reader picks up a thing or two, if my life could help someone in some way, it would not be such a bad thing. I don't expect every aspect of my life to be of interest to everyone, but I hope that everyone will find something of interest.

I must say, as I look back through the pages of my life, I can see that my experiences have been challenging, yet rewarding. I have memories as a boy of four collecting stamps, through the years in Anglo Chinese School (ACS) as a student and swimmer, then going abroad to pursue architecture and returning to be an architect. The years in Design Partnership, then DP Architects were also significant. Then from the 1970s through to the early 21st century, together with my collector friends, we put Singapore on the world map by establishing the Federation of Inter-Asian Philately (FIAP) and later in 1984 becoming a director of the Federation of International Philately (FIP) and rising to be its President from 2002 to 2006. From the 1990s I started being a patron to artists and collecting art, and my time with the National Gallery Singapore was yet another big chapter. It has been humbling, energising and instructive all at once. Would I do things differently if I could do them all over again? Probably not.

Maybe collecting historical documents and books relating to Singapore's history was what enabled me to stay sane while continuing these journeys, and I began to enjoy and learn from the processes. The subsequent donation of these documents to various institutions in Singapore was a final release and ending to my indulgent habit of collecting.

Through this book, the reader will learn that I am a firm believer in knowledge. I have been hungry to know more my entire life. The pursuit of knowledge is one of the cornerstones of my life. At every turn, it has been through knowledge that I have succeeded, it has been through knowledge that I have gained credibility, and it has been through knowledge that I have gained acceptance. Throughout my life, when I am armed with knowledge, I have no fear.

The other linchpin of my life has been my strong faith in teamwork. DP Architects, which I co-founded, considers teamwork to be one of my most important legacies for the firm. It is also important to me that I give credit when credit is due. Being an architect, I know the power of the team; it has never been through the work of just one person. Through the pages of this book, I hope this comes through, loud and clear.

This book would not have been possible without the support of my family, especially my wife Wen Gin, who has inspired me and made many suggestions throughout the past year. She helped me remember, went through the main events, checked the manuscript with the author, and sorted through a sea of photographs and pictures. I thank her for her tireless attention and care.

I have had a good life, never a dull moment; it has been eventful and mostly remarkable. And through many of these chapters in my life, I have felt God's hands guiding me. I am glad the author has decided to call the book *An Unfinished Canvas*. We learn and we continue this adventure called life for as long as we physically and mentally can. Life is what we make of it — my canvas is beautiful because I have dedicated my life to making it so.

Koh Seow Chuan
29 November 2023

Introduction

In August 2022, art collector Melvin Poh nudged me to write a book on Koh Seow Chuan. "Talk to him," he urged me. "You will not regret it," he promised.

I sent a message to Seow Chuan, and in October that year we had lunch in Tambuah Mas, an Indonesian restaurant in Tanglin Shopping Centre. Over delicious satay and nasi goreng, I got reacquainted with the man I had interviewed for my book on Lim Tze Peng, *Soul of Ink*, three years before.

I had a cursory knowledge of Seow Chuan — an architect, as well as a stamp and art collector. So I was in for quite a surprise, when in the ensuing months that followed, our weekly sessions would bring me through the life and times of a most unusual man. I entered worlds that I previously had no clue about, was told of a life few would have the opportunity or talent to experience. His has been a life whose passage began purposefully at the ripe young age of four. Interviewing him, with his wife Wen Gin listening and participating at his side, I began to have a new appreciation of architecture (how you use space), renewal (you want what you started to survive beyond you), collecting (the pleasure is in the knowledge) and teamwork (the whole is greater than the sum of its parts).

I chose the title, *An Unfinished Canvas*, after my first session with him. In an extraordinary life thus far, whether it is his career or his hobbies, he gives each a hundred and fifty percent, and he shines through every single one of them. As a student in Anglo Chinese School (ACS), he became the ACS chess champion and won the Dr Lim Kok Ann challenge trophy in 1956. The boy had a knack for turning adversity into opportunity. At age 10, a doctor noticed white patches at the bottom of his lungs and told him he was at higher risk for tuberculosis. He was encouraged to do more outdoor sports. So he followed in his brother's footsteps and took up swimming. The scrawny teenager soon became a swimming sensation, at one stage considered good enough for the Olympics. When he was 16, he broke the national record for the 100m backstroke at the Singapore National Championship. Then as an architect, he led the team building Esplanade — Theatres on the Bay, earning the firm the 2005 Royal Institute of British Architects' Worldwide Design Award and the 2006 President's Design Award Singapore. In the world of stamp-collecting, he won the Grand Prix National Award at the World Philatelic Exhibition held in Toronto Canada in 1996. In terms of art collecting, he had the biggest and most comprehensive collection of Nanyang pioneer artist Cheong Soo Pieng's work. Yet at 84, he tells me he has only finished two-thirds of his life. His canvas is unfinished.

I write this book to understand what makes someone like Seow Chuan tick. I conclude that he lived and continues to live his life guided by two principles, his strong belief in the power of knowledge, and the power of teamwork. And he discovered and started following these principles relatively early on in his life. Through stamps, he saw what knowledge could do for him academically and how it would always put him in a position of strength in whatever he did later in life. It was knowledge and his ability to lay hands on the right information that would see him through some of the biggest tests and challenges in his job and also in the various appointments he held after he retired. But it is in his absolute embrace of the power of many instead of one that sees him succeeding, project after project. People see in him a leader they rarely see in the world of architecture, the leader who insists on we over me, group glory over personal glory. The architecture firm he co-founded is more than 50 years old, now one of the biggest in the world.

What this book chronicles is not exhaustive, but they are the key activities of his life over eight decades. Through them, I hope the reader gets an idea of the spirit with which Seow Chuan approaches life. At 84, I detect raw forces beneath the aging exterior, unfinished trains of thought, and a man who though retired is far from retiring. "Lim Tze Peng is 103 and still painting," he says with a wink in his voice. "I am still a young man."

An extraordinary young man. Thank you, Melvin Poh, for the nudge. Yes, I have no regrets.

Woon Tai Ho

"Stamp collecting taught me that there was so much knowledge in the small humble stamp, that I have continued the quest of knowledge throughout my lifetime."

01

A Head Start in Life

"Stamps gave me an early start to real knowledge."

Chapter 1

A Head Start in Life

A Small Picture, a Window to the World

Koh Seow Chuan sees his life as a continuous painting. His is a vast canvas, and he is in no hurry to finish it. Gone are the initial pencil lines to guide him, the tentative strokes, the hesitant colours. Having added to the canvas over time — eight decades to be precise — he now sees a reasonably accomplished artwork before him. The strokes are full and confident, the colours bright yet subtle, the composition a mix of traditional lines and abstract glee. He is happy with what he sees, but wonders if he will ever finish the painting. As he adds finishing touches, each dab suggests another, each smudge a new possibility.

"What if I add a completely new layer of paint over it?" he asks himself whimsically. Over these eight decades, he has known and collected some of the best artists in Singapore and the region. The best artists don't stay stagnant or static; they evolve, they reinvent. "I may want my next layer to be abstract, or something that surprises. Isn't everything a work in progress? I am taking stock, thinking, reviewing. Even though I am slower physically, mentally I am still fast, still agile."

The brushes are not washed, the paints are still wet. The canvas heaves like a resting animal. Nothing is finished, everything is far from done.

We are seated in a Japanese restaurant facing the Keppel Marina, with a commanding view of private yachts against a brilliant blue sky. "Should we share or each order our own?" I ask.

"Let's share," he replies. As a rule of mine, I let the host determine the menu, for I am like a vacuum cleaner; I eat everything. The Kohs are endearingly cute as a couple. When Koh Seow Chuan talks to me about his life, he looks at his wife from time to time. It's a loving gesture. "At my age, I don't always remember everything," he lets out a throaty laugh. "So, I need my wife to verify the facts." Ah. A useful, loving gesture. His tone is thick, his enunciation crisp. At 84, he still has a very clear voice.

"How can I verify what you're saying when half of what you say I am hearing for the first time?" Wen Gin turns to me with a smile, her eyes dancing with mirth. "He assumes he has told me everything about his life. I am glad you are here. I am beginning to wonder if I know my husband at all, and we are both already retired."

Midday, the marina glistens. A knowing and easy comfort cushions their natter as the food arrives. Retiring and growing old together is a wish of many couples, but few get to live it. Along the way in life's journey, things can happen to either husband or wife. Fate needs to nod, luck needs to smile, and happily both parties need to know it requires commitment and a love that endures, year after year, decade after decade.

"When you reach your 70s and 80s together, at this point you have learned to accept each other almost completely. " Wen Gin lifts a piece of sashimi, puts it on her plate and looks up, "While we both had different careers, at home it has always been with this one person. The kids look at us as one and that's how we are to them and everyone else. Yes, we are lucky to have each other, as they say, in sickness and in health, and now, retired, we look forward to living a little differently. For instance, we bought a home to retire in, one to inspire us every day." Wen Gin has ordered sake for the table, but Seow Chuan prefers whisky. The alcohol seems to co-exist blissfully, a little like everything else with the Kohs.

"Our life starts when we remember it," Seow Chuan says philosophically. "The year I started to remember quite clearly was when I was a child of four. Like every boy that age, I loved to play, catching spiders, shooting other kids with rubber bands, collecting bottle caps. I was discovering, trying to make something out of nothing." There is a faraway look in his eyes. "But unlike most other kids, I was also 'playing' with something more serious than spiders and bottle caps, I was collecting stamps." He looks at his wife, then looks down as he takes a deep breath. "Stamps," he whispers as if to himself. "Each stamp was an adrenaline boost. They consumed me when I was a child, and all the way to my adult years and beyond. Each stamp may just be a small picture, but it was my window to the world. I was inspired to know what the world was like, and it got me dreaming about travelling to see the world in real life. Stamp collecting taught me that there was so much knowledge in the small humble stamp, that I have continued the quest of knowledge throughout my lifetime. You can say that stamps were my education outside of formal education. And I became a very good student because stamps gave me an early start to real knowledge."

The year was 1943, during the Japanese Occupation in Singapore. The only place his father, Koh Koon Yeow, went every morning was to his office, and at the end of the day, back home from the office. His company, Kim Bian Seng Company Limited, dealt in the trading of gold bullion, and had correspondences with China, Indonesia, Malaysia, and occasionally Europe. Though their network was small, it was gradually growing. Four-year-old Seow Chuan knew little of the goings-on in his father's office, but one aspect of the business that fascinated

Seow Chuan with father Koh Koon Yeow and mother Kang Tong Jin 1947.

him was the letters that arrived at the office.

After the Japanese Occupation period (1942—1945) more envelopes arrived as postal services opened up. "Each envelope had a stamp, or a few stamps, with a distinct postal marking," he says, his voice acquiring the wonder of a young child. "I was drawn into the stamps, the pictures, the colours. Every envelope came from another place, and I was told some came from far far away places. For me, they all told stories. Stories of monarchs, politicians, landscapes, wildlife, flora and fauna. My mind expanded beyond my physical space, beyond my young years. I started collecting without knowing what collecting was or entailed. I remember always looking out and waiting for the letters every time I was in my father's office."

Over time, the stamps got prettier and prettier, especially those from Europe. The young boy's mind was stimulated, he was captivated by how the pictures on the stamp spoke to him. That world of stamps was the equivalent of today's internet for him; they told of foreign adventures he would otherwise have not had any access to. Importantly, the language was visual, the beginning of how Seow Chuan saw his world, where everything unravelled visually. This visual aesthetic would go on to strongly influence his other pursuits, primarily his work in architecture and later his devotion to art.

"Between the ages of three to seven, you learn very fast. And when I knew what I could learn from stamps I became very anxious to learn. It was the beginning of real knowledge, and I grew to understand the importance and power of knowledge. For example, I learnt about royalty from a stamp with a monarch. Countries without royalty came up with people who contributed in other ways, like scientists or politicians. There were stamps that depicted landscapes, like Switzerland. It was a never-ending visual buffet. My eyes feasted and I was in rapture."

Stamps also taught the young boy the concepts of method and system. Even from that tender age, he developed his own personal approach to collecting: by countries, by subject matter and by what he considered to be unusual and important. Over time, he started to treat every stamp like a person he respected; he let each stamp speak to him. This respect he accorded stamps would stay with him and influence him in everything else he did. "I let the stamps, or the postal markings, talk to me and inform me how they'd like to be treated. Later, when I started to collect art, I did and still do collect in this same way. I also practise architecture by considering context and site location. In architecture, I often spend time at the site mulling, until I get the message I need about what kind of building should sit on it."

Seow Chuan is the youngest in a big family of 11 children. His older brothers took notice of what the youngest in the family was doing. "My second brother saw the potential of stamp collecting as a business. He was so interested that he started a company. When I was 10 years old, he asked me to help him in his stamp company."

The brother's company was registered as the *Universal Stamp Company*; the 10-year-old played a pivotal role, valuing the stamps while his brother marketed them. By then, Singapore was under British administration. In colonial Singapore, the study and collecting of stamps, philately, was predominantly a hobby of the wealthy, which meant mainly among the British. There were very few locals who had the wealth or knowledge to be in the stamp collecting circle.

"Initially I did not know other local collectors. But I later found out that there were some very serious and big Chinese collectors," Seow Chuan leans back onto his chair. "I got to know one of them, Martin Lee, in the late 1940s and early 50s. In the early 60s when I returned from Melbourne, having completed my architecture degree, we communicated more. As architects, some of our activities converged. He came from a well-to-do family and owned a company called *Lee and Fletcher*. Our friendship developed and deepened over the decades. When People's Park Complex was completed, he bought a shop there and we continued to meet."

As the collecting continued, Seow Chuan did not realise how valuable his own collection was, or how knowledgeable he had become as a collector. "I never knew I was a 'somebody' until quite late. When I started working, when I earned money, I started to make some real sacrifices, by putting a lot of money into stamps. Everyone around me started to realise I was becoming a serious collector. I even borrowed money to buy stamps. But it wasn't mindless or reckless. I was guided and instructed by knowledge, deep knowledge, and my confidence was high. People around took notice of how meticulous I was, how collaborative I was and how disciplined I had become."

This discipline, of working on and collecting based on knowledge would typify Seow Chuan's approach in almost everything else he did. Even when he played chess and billiards, or swam competitively later in life, the attitude and approach to these games mirrored the same focus, the same cognitive understanding, that nothing in life would be worth pursuing, if each was not accompanied by the same rigour and passion that accompanied his stamp collecting.

Academically he was always among the top. "I attribute a lot of my academic success to the discipline instilled when I was young. Coupled with a parallel 'education' stamp collecting offered, it was a head start in life. To give you an example, my parents took me away for seven months to visit Kulangsu in Amoy, China (now known as Gulangyu in Xiamen, China), and for two months to Hong Kong because I topped my class in primary one and was given a double promotion."

The Japanese, the British and Independence

Although there was widespread jubilation following the Japanese surrender in 1945, the sense of triumph was soon replaced by a sobering atmosphere as Singapore's immediate post-war years were marked by pressing social and welfare needs. Living conditions were appalling as the problems of overcrowding continued after the war, forcing families to live in crammed and filthy slums and squatters that had poor ventilation and lacked proper sanitation. Acute shortages of food and healthcare plagued the population, which was also threatened by outbreaks of fire and diseases due to poor living conditions and overcrowded spaces.[1]

"This period saw the brewing of an early national consciousness," Seow Chuan says as he sits up and casts his mind back to his childhood and teenage years. "With the image of the all-powerful Western imperialists shattered in World War Two, the widespread social and welfare problems in post-war Singapore soon became sources of discontent that fuelled the spread of political agitation against the colonial government. Young, educated members of the disaffected class began to organise themselves, coming together to discuss the shortcomings of the government and plan their course of action, with the ultimate goal being for Singapore to break away from colonial rule." It was under such a climate of political awakening that Singapore's constitutional development got underway, as the British took cautious steps to introduce greater local participation in government elections from 1948 to 1959.

Stamps were another form of 'currency', facilitating internal and

---

[1] "Singapore and its road to independence after World War II", *Facts and Details* https://factsanddetails.com/southeast-asia/Singapore/sub5_7a/entry-3713.html.

external communications. Today, stamps on envelopes are regarded as snail mail, but in those days, especially before telecommunications, stamped mail was the only trusted and credible form of contact between two locations, even though some mail from overseas would take several months to arrive. For a stamp collector, the stamp designs during this period couldn't have been more compelling: from the Japanese to colonial administration, from British rule to eventual self-rule, stamps were a visual documentation of the various occupations and administrations.

"Our family had businesses in Southeast Asia, Hong Kong and China," Seow Chuan leans forward as his head tilts back a little. "Stamps from these periods, the 40s, 50s and 60s, showed the dramatic political changes and developments of the region, and of Singapore: from the Japanese period to the British, then to self-rule, where I played a role in the design of post-independent stamps."

Seow Chuan's father Koh Koon Yeow came to Singapore with his father Koh Boon Mua, who had four brothers. His grandfather was an astute businessman who knew he needed to leave China as it was politically unstable. For Koh Boon Mua, the best chance to keep his wealth and continue to make money was to spread out his family members in Southeast Asia. So, one was stationed in Penang, one in Kuala Lumpur, one in Bangkok, one in Surabaya, and two in Singapore, all engaged in the melting and trading of precious metals, the gold and silver bullion business.

When he made enough money, he went back to China in the 1930s and bought several properties in Amoy and a house in Kulangsu. "It is a pedestrian-only island off the coast of Amoy, Fujian Province in southern China," Seow Chuan's voice stirs. He sits up and leans forward. Kulangsu obviously means something special to him. "Now a UNESCO

World Cultural Heritage Site, the island is only two square kilometres in area, and one can get there by an eight-minute ferry ride from downtown Xiamen. In 1947 there were only about 20,000 people living on the island, but today it is a major domestic tourist destination, attracting more than 10 million visitors per year, making it one of China's most visited tourist attractions. Gulangyu not only bans cars, but also bicycles. The only vehicles permitted are small electric buggies and electric government service vehicles."

Wen Gin's calm face turns towards me, "The island is known as the piano island because every home has a piano." Her voice sustains a quiet excitement. "The island is a unique place that dares to retain its uniqueness."

"When the Communist Party took over," Seow Chuan looks down, his voice slowing, "the rules changed, almost everything was suddenly owned by the state. In 1947 my father went back to China to take stock of my grandfather's assets; but he did not do it fast enough. We had a shipping company, properties, we even co-owned a bank in Hong Kong. Most of what we owned, factories and properties went, except the house in Kulangsu. I was determined not to lose the Kulangsu house. To me, that was my grandfather's legacy. He had worked so hard there and contributed in his own way to what the island had become. The place is something his children and grandchildren needed to know, this special and unusual part of China's history and how the family fitted in that history." He fixes his gaze on me. "It took me 15 years to claim back the house."

While the political developments in China were brutally momentous, the changes in Southeast Asia worked out much better for the Kohs. This was particularly so for Seow Chuan's stamp journey; the gods were smiling down on him. As the dark clouds of the war parted, the bright sun rays took special care, exposing the collector not just to national but also international fame. "When I graduated from university, and started to work professionally, and I earned money," he pauses, trying to find the right word for making a reasonably good salary, "for the first time I had my own money to buy stamps. My cousin, Khor Seow Hong, was 32 then, and one of the biggest stamp collectors and hoarders in Singapore and Southeast Asia at that time. His business needed his full attention, and he wanted to expand that business. He knew if he were to focus on his business, he needed to end his obsession with stamps, and hand over his special collection to someone who would not only take good care of it but would also benefit from having it." He stops, turning first to his wife then me. "I bought over the whole collection."

His wife smiles broadly as she throws her head back. "Of course. Again, I am hearing this for the first time."

Seow Chuan continues, "We negotiated amicably, he knew he was handing the collection to someone who would value it, so the terms didn't hurt me even though it was a large purchase. He allowed me to pay by instalments over a few years. For me, it was a great opportunity." He looks at me now, and I suspect he is leaving the best part of the story to the very last. "It was a hoard, and like all hoards, a lot of it was common, or many of the same kind. But there were also some rare diamonds among the rocks." Seow Chuan had only been 22 years old then, and buying the collection pushed him up to a whole new league. In essence, what he had bought was over 20 years of knowledge other collectors could only dream of. Suddenly Koh Seow Chuan was fast-tracked into a lane few collectors could reach in their lifetime, never mind a young man only in his early 20s.

But the collector is quick to remind me that stamp collecting is not about one-time buyouts or big purchases. It requires the collector to be on a constant lookout, and the collection needs daily nourishment. "I visited post offices often, to collect special stamps and interesting postmarks to continue to learn and acquire knowledge."

By his mid 20s, he was probably the most knowledgeable collector in the region. He continued with small and big purchases, prudently in his books because he knew what to buy; but extravagantly to those who did not know. "I was always cash-strapped, especially in the early years. A typical ferocious collector, asset-rich but cash-poor!"

While the philately world was huge, it was also a well-networked and closely-knit community. After the big purchase from his cousin, he started getting noticed, started attracting attention. Other collectors were curious. Who was this young collector? How had he gotten hold of such a collection? People started reaching out to him. "There were three contacts that were very valuable," Seow Chuan shifts in his seat again. I sense his stamp empire was set to get even bigger. "One was in Kuala Lumpur, the collector had accumulated stacks and stacks, from during the Japanese Occupation and also the British administration period. He was growing old, and he wanted to exit. I was working in Kuala Lumpur then. The Malayan Architects Co-Partnership (MAC) had posted me there. In 1963, I bought the whole lot off him." The second contact was Tay Tian Song, a Singaporean who had collected stamps for a long time, since the Japanese Occupation. "He was astute and managed to get hold of a large quantity of Japanese Occupation stamps. I bought bulks from him, four bulk-purchases altogether." A pause now. He is taking his time with the third contact.

"The third case was rather tricky," he laughs. "This person, in Kota Bahru, Kelantan, knew the value of what he had, and wasn't willing to sell. My mother's youngest sister married a medical doctor and settled there. I was introduced to him by my cousin. He had a biscuit tin of

Japanese covers, about 50 or 60 envelopes in there. I knew this because I had a friend in the United States named Milo Rowell who had told me about him. What he had was worth about S$500 each. I persuaded my friend Milo to buy the whole group of covers together. In those days, you could buy a terrace house with that money."

A collector's world is an obsessive and absorbing one. The collection is good but never quite good enough. You stand tall, but someone else is always taller. As your network gets stronger, you stretch yourself thinner. The word 'enough' is not in a collector's vocabulary. It is a bit like someone jumping on a ferocious tiger, and not knowing how to get off without being bitten. "I was always cash-poor and asset-rich," he says, letting out a breath of air. "For a large part of my life then I had been walking on a tightrope where it concerned cash. Thankfully, I had a good reputation, I was known to be upright and honest. I never failed anyone and I always delivered. Many people were prepared to loan me money. The CEO of a Hong Kong bank told me, 'Whenever you need money, come to me. You pledge your stamps to me, put them in my safe deposit box. Just tell me how much you want.' That was the level of trust I had with my friends and business partners. Later, when my company DP Architects had a dire cash flow problem, I did precisely that. I pledged my stamps for cash. A person's integrity and reputation are of utmost importance. Whatever I had agreed on, I had honoured, and the banker knew he could trust me as long as sufficient collateral was placed with the bank."

Public Service Star at 31

We are now in the bright living room of Seow Chuan's home. He has chosen to sit with his back to the sliding doors. Wen Gin decides to pull the day curtains halfway across, reducing the amount of morning light dramatically.

"You get such good morning light," I say as my eyes scan his walls. There are unusual Cheong Soo Pieng sketches hung here. Most of Seow Chuan's art collection is, of course, famously stored at Helutrans where he occasionally shows them to his close friends. The few paintings and artworks hung here have been selected for special reasons. There is an unusual oil painting of sunflowers by Lim Tze Peng.

"If you asked Lim Tze Peng about this, he would probably not remember," Seow Chuan laughs. "He rarely paints in oil anymore, and this had been his only attempt at sunflowers. My wife loves sunflowers, so she asked for this painting to be brought out of storage when we moved into the apartment."

We will have time to talk about art later. Now I want to continue his stamp adventure, and how stamps led him to his first award, the Public Service Star, at a ripe young age of 31.

First, a fascinating stamp story.

A letter or parcel from one side of the earth can reach the other within a day by cargo flight. The stamps on the letter may have circled the globe, but when they reach the recipient, they would still be in their good original condition. Now cast your mind back to the days of the Second World War.

Singapore was occupied by the Japanese between 1942 and 1945. A postal service was established by the Japanese military administration for the needs of the local population, the soldiers as well as the prisoners-of-war (POWs) in Singapore. For British POWs in particular, mail from the British Islands to the prisoner-of-war camp in Singapore was delivered in several stages via many countries. Such correspondence was free to senders and was initially forwarded to the military censorship office in London, from where it was returned to the post office. Then the mail was sent to Tehran, from there to Moscow, from Moscow by train on the Trans-Siberian Railway to China, then by the Chinese-Eastern Railway to the Korean port of Busan, from there by sea to the Japanese city of Shimonoseki and finally by land to Tokyo. At the last stage, letters were transported by sea to Singapore and then delivered to Changi Prison. A long, long journey, the mail was in transit for more than a year, not to mention the eventual condition of the stamps and envelopes! The letters and postcards of the POWs were limited to 25 words, and their content was also inspected by the Japanese administration.[2]

If only stamps could talk! How they were treated in the hands of the various postmen, post-office clerks, their experiences in the air, by sea and on land, the changes of weather, seasons… What they had been through can only be imagined.

Stamps are also a chronicle of history. In 1946, the British Military Administration began and lasted until 1948. Singapore became a crown colony in 1948 and the first stamps of Singapore were issued on 1 September 1948. They were similar to stamps of the Straits Settlements, but inscribed with SINGAPORE at the foot. From 3 June 1959, Singapore became a self-governing state as the State of Singapore. Five sets of commemorative stamps were issued during this period, to mark

[2] Wikipedia, Japanese Occupation, Postage stamps and postal history of Singapore.

the New Constitution in 1959 and National Day in 1960, 1961, 1962, and 1963. All were inscribed State of Singapore. Beginning in 1960, the portrait of the British crown no longer appeared on the Singapore postal miniatures. In 1962, the post office began issuing a new standard series of stamps depicting orchids, fish and birds that were native to Singapore, without the portrait of the Queen.[3]

A total of 73 postage stamps were issued in colonial and self-governing Singapore between 1948 and 1963. On 16 September 1963, Singapore briefly merged with the Federation of Malaya along with Sabah and Sarawak to form the Federation of Malaysia. On 9 August 1965, Singapore was expelled and became a sovereign independent republic. A set of stamps, featuring four clasped hands, was issued in 1966 to commemorate the first anniversary of independence, marked Republic of Singapore, but all later stamps to the present day have been marked just Singapore.

"The late 50s and early 60s were defining moments for stamps in Singapore," Seow Chuan declares quietly. "I joined the Singapore Stamp Club in 1963. I was up-to-date and probably the most knowledgeable there. Many members were keen to know what I had. When I had many of the same, I shared with them. I believe in enhancing knowledge, that was my compass. I befriended and shared with collectors and I always believed in teamwork. I didn't want to be collecting alone. If there was a team, with a broad base of collectors, that would improve the hobby."

He takes a sip of the black coffee Wen Gin has made. His voice has a relentless patience, one word marching after another. "In the Stamp Club, there were two students who had a thirst for knowledge. One

---

[3] *Stanley Gibbons Stamp Catalogue: Commonwealth and British Empire Stamps* 1840-1970. 110th edition. London: Stanley Gibbons, 2008, pp.527-529.

was studying in Anglo Chinese School, and one in Raffles Institution — Hong Tuck Kun and Chua Eu Tiong. Both did well academically and went on to do very well professionally, one in DBS Bank and the other as an oncologist. In 1963 and 1964, these students would come to me, and they'd take 13 to 15 stacks, for a dollar each. It lifts me to see young students keen on acquiring and sharing knowledge. Over time, my popularity grew in The Stamp Club, and in 1968 I replaced a European to be its President. At that time, this was a unique phenomenon, for a Caucasian man to be replaced by a local. I was the President for 10 years."

At the Singapore Stamp Club, he cultivated a group of passionate collectors, among whom were Chan Huei Lock and later Tay Peng Hian. When he retired as President of the Stamp Club in 1977, Chan Huei Lock succeeded him as President and remained in that role until 1988. "To make sustainable improvements to the hobby, succession planning also crept into my stamp hobby. Like with my architectural practice, I nurtured new leaders who could take over, so that I could pursue new interests."

With Singapore's independence in 1965, the newly formed government looked for local talent to spearhead developments in various fields, and naturally Seow Chuan, as the President of The Stamp Club, caught their eye. In 1968, then Minister for Communications Yong Nyuk Lin approached Seow Chuan to set up the Stamp Advisory Committee. While the committee's leader was a political appointee, Seow Chuan chaired one of the committees for stamp design. "I was clear that we needed to project a confident Singapore," he remembers with quiet assertion. "We wanted to project Singapore to the world, an independent country now. We wanted to begin to create institutions to run our own affairs. We discussed and talked about how to design and print the stamps. I submitted several papers to the government on

Singapore 150th Anniversary Stamp Exhibition 1969. Mural Symbol of Growth and Globalisation. Koh Seow Chuan and Phua Bah Lee.

Opening speech by Minister Yong Nyuk Lin.

the topic of how to revamp our postal services. While we build high rises, we also need to consider nature, the natural habitat of the island. So, our environment and tropical climate were important. The first major series of stamps for everyday use depicted our flora and fauna, done in an abstract way. It was iconic. We had a panel of Singaporean designers, including graphic designers and artists. The next important series was the 150th Anniversary of the founding of Singapore in 1969. The designs depicted four stages of Singapore, from a swamp village to the Japanese Occupation, then the British Administration, and finally Independence. A national stamp exhibition was held in 1969. The theme was 'From Singapore to the World'. The poster design showed how we radiated to the region and then to the world. This had, of course, not yet happened then. It was mine and my team's subconscious ambition. Little did we know it would eventually be realised, and fulfilled in such a big and grand way — Singapore the metropolis."

The *Bintang Bakti Masyarakat* or Public Service Star is a Singaporean decoration instituted in 1963. It is awarded to any person who has rendered valuable public service to the people of Singapore, or who has distinguished themselves in the field of arts and letters, sports, the sciences, business, the professions or the labour movement. The first recipients included a future president of Singapore, S.R. Nathan, who received the Public Service Star in 1964. When Minister Yong Nyuk Lin recommended Seow Chuan for the award in 1971, he was probably one of the youngest to be put forward, only 31 years old then. "When I received the award, I knew it was an honour. The award was presented by President (Benjamin) Sheares, and I remember feeling proud when he pinned the medal on my lapel. It has been half a century, more than 50 years ago. When I look at the medal today, I am filled with warmth and also a sense of incredulity. I was only 31."

What he did for Singapore attracted international attention. Together with other philately enthusiasts, Seow Chuan helped to officially establish the Inter-Asia Philatelic Federation, later known as Federation of Inter-Asian Philately (FIAP) in 1974. "The FIAP was actually founded and registered in Singapore. I held the position of General Secretary. It was a milestone for Singapore philately, a recognition that Singapore stamp collectors have reached international standards. This paved the way for Singapore to join the world body, the Federation of International Philately, FIP, in 1978."

The international light continued to shine on Seow Chuan; in 1984 he was elected to the FIP Board of Directors at its Madrid Congress in Spain. "I replaced an incumbent who was German. I was careful, such an accomplishment might have provoked spiteful envy if it wasn't worn with modesty. I remember telling myself, I have to be humble and low key. I did not want to create any ripples. I was there to see what I could do, how I could contribute. In 1998 I was the Vice President. In 2002 I was elected as the President of the FIP Board. I was the second Asian President and stayed as President for four years."

Most stamp collectors focus on stamps of their own country or region. Seow Chuan's stamp collecting interest was global. His Perak and Jaipur Collections won him Gold Medals, while his Straits Settlements Revenue Collection won him a Large Gold. Seow Chuan also holds the distinction of being the first Singaporean to sign the British Philatelic Federation's Roll of Distinguished Philatelists in 1992. "This was created in the early 1920s to recognise great philatelists in the world, and the first signatory was King George V. Each year not more than five philatelists in the world were invited to sign. As of today, there are less than 800 philatelists who have signed and less than 150 of them are alive. It was a great honour for me and also a great honour for Singapore."

Koh Seow Chuan holds the distinction of being the first Singaporean to sign the British Philatelic Federation's Roll of Distinguished Philatelists in 1992.

1995 was a significant milestone in Seow Chuan's philatelic journey and a proud moment for Singapore. As the vice president of the Singapore '95 organising committee, he lent his philatelic expertise and network to successfully host Singapore's first ever World Stamp Exhibition, organised with the support of SingPost under the patronage of FIP, with more than 3,000 frames of competitive exhibits on display over ten days. It was one of the biggest stamp shows ever held in Singapore. Singapore had finally arrived on the philatelic world stage. The little red dot went on to host two more world stamp shows, in 2004 and 2015. Today, members of Singapore Stamp Club regularly participate in world stamp exhibitions with confidence, often winning awards that would make any country proud.[4]

In 1996, his collection of stamps issued in New Brunswick and Nova Scotia between 1851 and 1867 earned him the Grand Prix National Award at the World Philatelic Exhibition in Canada. He was the first Singaporean to win an international stamp-collecting award in North America.

"After winning these international awards, and having served as president of FIP for four years (2002—2006), in 2006, I decided that I should reduce my time and energy spent on stamp collecting," Seow Chuan says matter-of-factly. "I was already in my 60s, and I have had a fantastic run and a terrific time. Stamps have taught me so much. In life, one needs to know when to begin and also, when to end. I began to slow down with stamps. It coincided with the time when I was asked to look at turning the City Hall and Supreme Court into the National Gallery Singapore. To me, this call to play a national and pivotal role in the arts was more important than remaining president of FIP. Therefore, I accepted the appointment of deputy chairman of the Steering Committee in 2005 and executive chairman for the Development of the National Gallery in 2007, and did not seek re-election in FIP. In fact, I had already planned my succession there."

By this time, Seow Chuan's stamp collecting team had expanded to include many more collectors including Tay Peng Hian, Daniel Teo and Professor Cheah Jin Seng. Tay Peng Hian was made president of the FIAP in the 1980s. He received numerous international philatelic awards, and was president of the FIP between 2010 and 2018. "Daniel Teo succeeded me as chairman of the Singapore Philatelic Museum in 2009 and Prof Cheah Jin Seng succeeded him in 2013. His influence

[4] SSC Newsletter, 80th Anniversary Edition. *Koh Seow Chuan — Vanguard of Philately* by Dennis Chua & KC Koh.

overflowed to neighbouring Southeast Asian countries such as Thailand, Philippines, Indonesia and Malaysia."

It was clear Singapore had been put onto the philately world map and accorded immense respect and admiration. International stamp institutions and the collecting fraternity had seen the work of Singaporean collectors like Seow Chuan and believed in putting Singaporean collectors in leadership positions in world philately. "It was with great pride that Singaporean collector Tay Peng Hian was elected for two terms, eight years altogether, as the president of FIP, from 2011 to 2019, and an Australian national succeeded him from 2019 to 2023. The current FIP president is a Thai national, and another Singaporean collector, Richard Tan, is on the FIP board."

In the world of stamps, Koh Seow Chuan was soaring on so many levels; he had stamps to thank for a head start in life. Now it was time he tended to the other gardens in his mind. The boy who held his first stamp on an envelope at four was now a distinguished architect and a father of four children and five grandchildren. The small picture on each stamp was indeed his window to the big world awaiting him. After his tenure as FIP president, the philately world started to look at Singapore with much admiration and respect.

"I was drawn to architecture from a very young age, I saw that I can affect humanity at a very fundamental level."

02

People's Park Complex

First 'City Room'

GOLDEN KEY

Chapter 2

People's Park Complex

"The reality of the building does not consist of the roof and walls, but the space within to be lived."

Lao Tzu

A Calling

If art is the expression of human creative skill and imagination, architecture gives this expression its form and function. To Koh Seow Chuan, architecture encompasses every aspect of human activity: whether a person is resting or working, sleeping or awake, he exists and functions within the fabric of the structure that supports him. "I was drawn to architecture from a very young age, I saw that I could affect humanity at a very fundamental level. I grew up during a momentous time, from the Japanese Occupation, to colonial rule, then when a country got its independence. I associated architecture with *building*, in its metaphorical and actual sense, that we would *rebuild* the country from an occupied state to an independent country."

And from the very start, architecture has never just been about the visual look of a building or structure, but about the space and how the space is understood. "It is the spirit of the space that triggers an inspiration. Because of its all-encompassing nature, architecture is the mother of all the visual arts. It is something that when you create it, lasts longer than any of the other art forms. Why am I an architect? Architecture gives me a chance to be a practitioner of how people work, how people live. And it is a profession that can inspire lives and uplift the human spirit. Our time in the world is limited and short. So, we have to live it in the best possible way."

Sitting in his living room on a Friday morning, Seow Chuan is quietly excited to relive the birth of his architectural journey. Wen Gin is a meticulous chronicler of his career; she has 30 volumes of photographs, brochures, newspaper cuttings, and documents spanning almost half a century of his illustrious career. With a laugh that sounds like a cough, Seow Chuan says he wants to start at the beginning and talk about the architect who has inspired him more than anyone else, Frank Lloyd Wright.

The year was 1935, and the US was in the midst of the Great Depression. Edgar J. Kaufmann, a department store magnate, and his wife, Liliane, commissioned Wright to design a weekend retreat on their family's land near the former Bear Run community southeast of Pittsburgh. The Kaufmanns expected a weekend house that would offer views of a favourite waterfall. They were shocked by Wright's bold vision of placing their home directly above the waterfall.

"He did not want to relegate the falls to a mere view, one that the Kaufmanns might occasionally look at from afar," Seow Chuan says with a knowing look in his eyes. "Instead, he wanted to bring the falls into the family's everyday life, to bring the outside in. The Kaufmanns would always be able to hear the movement of the water and be aware of the waterfall's presence. Frank Lloyd Wright helped pioneer the concept of organic architecture, with interiors and exteriors in balanced harmony. Embodying this philosophy, the house could be compared to a living organism with all parts relating to the whole, making form and function wholly intertwined."

The construction of *Fallingwater* began in 1935 and the Kaufmanns moved in towards the end of 1937. Wright sought to integrate humans, architecture, and nature together so that each one would be improved by the relationship. *Fallingwater* accordingly grew from the site's rocky landscape; its concrete terraces floated above the falls, drawing attention to the water while respecting its space. Wright intended the circulation of the building to have a sense of compression when indoors, and of expansion when approaching the outdoors. Hence the expansive terraces occupied about half of the building while the interior spaces were small with low ceilings, creating a sheltered cave amid the rugged landscape. *Time* magazine featured Wright and a drawing of the building on the cover of its 17 January 1938 issue.[1]

"Wright's philosophy of creating environments that were both functional and humane is what I subscribe to," says Seow Chuan slowly, his voice thoughtful. "I focus not only on a building's appearance but how it would connect with and enrich the lives of those inside it. *Fallingwater* blends beautifully into its natural surroundings, both drawing from and contributing to the setting. Wright's architecture showcases materials like wood and stone in their authentic state, rather than twisting them into something new, a trend that continues today."

The American architect was an admirer of Oriental philosophy and instructed by Lao Tzu's concept of vacuum, or negative space, that only in the vacuum lay what is truly essential. There is a famous saying of his: *The reality of a room was to be found in the vacant space enclosed by*

---

[1] "AD Classics: Fallingwater House / Frank Lloyd Wright" by Adelyn Perez. *ArchDaily*, www.archdaily.com.

the roof and walls, not in the roof and walls themselves.[2] One could mould clay into a vessel for instance, but it is the emptiness within that creates the usefulness of the vessel. "When an architect is given a site, he needs to understand the space the site offers first, and not be distracted by other details." Seow Chuan looks at my face and smiles. "The space above the waterfall was for Wright more useful than the view it offered. What Lao Tzu expounded inspired me, as it did Wright. I was simultaneously also inspired by the Swiss French architect Le Corbusier, whose use of concrete and leaving it in its natural state influenced me tremendously. I must also include German American architect Mies van der Rohe, whose building structures were essentially made of steel and glass, characterised by minimal uses of industrial materials, calling his buildings 'skin and bones', and his by now infamous expression 'less is more'."

Architects aside, I am interested to know if there was a building that, when he walked in, made him want to be the architect that he eventually became. Was there a dwelling or building that actually changed his life?

He looks up, his eyes wide like an exclamation mark. "In Tokyo," he says without hesitation, "the Yoyogi National Gymnasium was designed by Kenzo Tange to house the swimming and diving events for the 1964 Summer Olympics. As I always say, in architecture, it is how a good building uplifts the human spirit. The gymnasium is what I would call a perfect hybridization of western modernist aesthetics and traditional Japanese architecture. Tange designed the sporting complex with a dynamic form that resembled a desert tent or the very native Japanese pagoda. I wanted a chance to be there as I was a

[2] *The Whirling Arrow, News and updates from the Frank Lloyd Wright Foundation. The Space Within: Part 4, Sense of Space. The Book of Tao.*

competitive swimmer, and sure enough, it evoked an overwhelming feeling in me. Although I was coming to the tail end of my swimming career, the gymnasium injected my being with an intense sense of power, and I told myself, maybe I should continue swimming, I should push myself further. In ACS, the motto is, *The Best Is Yet to Be*, and that was exactly how I felt, one of those moments when you feel you can do anything. Few buildings empower me the way the gymnasium did. It came to symbolise the games and more than that, along with the bullet train, it came to epitomise the re-emergence of Japan as a modern industrial and technological power. No other piece of architecture succeeds in embodying the spirit of Japan's post war period of high economic growth in such a remarkable manner."

Seow Chuan's love affair with Japanese architecture has deep roots. When he was a young architect with Malayan Architects Co-Partnership, one of the founders, Lim Chong Keat, sent him to Japan in 1966 where he got to know the legendary Fumihiko Maki, who studied under Kenzo Tange, both recipients of the prestigious Pritzker Architecture Prize. Early in Maki's career, he became a founding member of an avant-garde group of talented young Japanese architects calling themselves Metabolists. Metabolism was an architectural movement originating in Japan in the late 1950s, which suggested that architectural megastructures should model themselves after nature and that designed buildings and cities should emulate living beings with a continuous cycle of growth and change rather than being mere static entities. Metabolism promoted a dynamic city and flexible architecture that could meet the needs of an ever-changing environment. Metabolist architects felt that the static structures created after World War II in Japan had a limited lifespan.[3]

[3] "The Metabolism Movement — The Promised Tokyo" by Lucas Moreno, sabukaru.online.

"The concept of a city room was reinforced by Maki," says Seow Chuan in a reflective tone. "He thought cities of the world lacked communal spaces where people could interact and cross-fertilise. His idea of large rooms in enclosed urban spaces allowing a network of pedestrian circulation left a deep impression on me. It would instruct how we conceptualised one of the first big buildings I was involved in, the porous People's Park Complex."

The trip happened more than 50 years ago, yet somehow his interactions with Maki seemed to be etched in his mind. "Maki introduced me to many of his staff, one of whom later came to lecture in Singapore. He also brought me to see many pioneer architects, including Kunio Maekawa, who designed the Tokyo Metropolitan. Kunio Maekawa designed some aesthetically powerful buildings with huge roofs, the space below partly enclosed and partly exposed." Seow Chuan takes in a deep breath and leans back, allowing his physical body time to catch up with his mind. "I would visit Maki at 10 in the morning, by 12 noon he would say, 'Let's go for lunch.' We went for lunch below a bridge by the highway. They had these stalls, and we ate there, food on skewers, typically Japanese, very spontaneous, very communal. It was their way of life, all integrated. There was no me and you, 'I am a senior you are a pupil' interaction. Everyone was an equal. That informed me. That trip to Japan opened my eyes not just to good Japanese architecture, but also the civic culture of Japanese architects. Maki was a pioneer Metabolist, I grew to appreciate it as a kind of humanism as well. One needs to stay humble in order to learn, otherwise you stop learning and think you already know everything. Maki and I have stayed friends for more than half a century."

It could have started with his stamp collecting, reinforced by his days in Monk's Hill Primary and ACS Secondary, for Seow Chuan makes it a point to remind himself to stay humble, be compassionate, and be a team player. These could very easily be motherhood statements, words only, with no resonance in action. But Seow Chuan has embedded them as guidelines into all his endeavours and made them part and parcel of his work; over the years they became values that formed the premises that serve his life.

"Even early in my childhood, I witnessed life's adversities and sufferings triggered by the Japanese Occupation. I saw how important it was to be kind and compassionate. I told myself that when I grew up, my work had to help alleviate suffering. In architecture, I found that I could live a creative and compassionate life; I saw it as my calling. I am influenced not just by architects but more importantly by humanitarians like Albert Schweitzer. Recognizing that he was born to privilege, Schweitzer made the decision to dedicate his life to the service of others when he turned 30. That kind of selflessness moves me."

But being humble is not easy, especially when architects are involved in huge projects. Seow Chuan witnessed many instances in his early years where architects let their egos get the better of them. "In architecture, when we deal with projects that are big, public and are often in the eye of the media, you often see ugly egos at play. So, you hear architects saying, 'This is my project, that is my project. I am the architect.' Architecture is the ultimate form of collaborative work. When Malayan Architects Co-Partnership was dissolved, we formed Design Partnership in 1967. The structure of the firm, even the name itself, highlighted that Design Partnership was formed as a collective rather than as a singular principal design studio. From the beginning, the firm's practice was founded on teamwork: talented and committed individuals who would strive towards excellence together. We eschewed the concept of the Master Architect, all members of each project contributed to the design development of a building. And it carries through to the present, where DP Architects is pluralistic in nature and without a fixed design aesthetic."

He leans back, letting a deep breath out, not a sigh, but remembering something good. "I had good training being a team player. If you look at my year books in ACS, I was the captain of the chess team, captain of the swimming team, founding chairman of the stamp club, all while in ACS. When you hold those positions, your biggest role is to rally and motivate the team. And over the years, I learnt that teamwork is the most effective path to success."

Being a leader has taught him something basic about how each person can be motivated to do their best. "Every human being born into this world is unique, in the sense that he has certain abilities, and certain disabilities. There are certain things he can do well, and certain things he can't do well. We are not born with equal or the same talents." His voice is steady, and he moves his left arm up to support his face. "That being the case, the only equal thing that every human being has in common is, each is equal in being able to exercise the decision to be what he wants to be, and in that, he can be the best, given the innate faculties and abilities he is born with. And I think possibly my education in Monk's Hill School and later in ACS enforced that, because the ACS motto is *The Best is Yet to Be*. That establishes a base, that from beginning to end, you continue to improve yourself, to learn, to be the best that you can be. Life and learning are a journey. Learning never ends, it ends only when you die."

The First Mall

1967 was an important year for Koh Seow Chuan. It marked the dissolution of Malayan Architects Co-Partnership (MAC) in April, and the formation of a new firm in May.

"William Lim, one of the founders of MAC, approached Tay Kheng Soon and I to continue working together with the same collaborative spirit under a new name, Design Partnership." Seow Chuan's voice betrays no emotion. "The three of us would have equal footing as founding partners. It would be run like a collaborative, a co-partnership the way MAC was meant to be, was supposed to be, but failed to be." Subsequently, Design Partnership was dissolved in 1975, and a new architecture company known as DP Architects Pte Ltd was established, one he would work in for the rest of his career in architecture.

"Ha, the early days," he lets out a laugh. "They were good days. Formed two years after Singapore's independence, we were young, ambitious and optimistic and we believed in the power of architecture to lay the foundation of our country and to change the world. The very act of building was a positive step towards creating a new future apart from its colonial past. But the business reality of day-to-day existence was brutal and humbling at the beginning. We were all very poor, we didn't have money. The first few months none of us received a salary. While we waited for big projects, we needed bread and butter work, so the first project was designing British Petroleum (BP) service stations. We did the layout for their pumps, workshops and 7-Eleven facilities. I remember running it with one technical member of staff, construction for it was also very quick. I also worked on small building projects and renovation works for relatives and friends. That was real bread and butter. We needed both small and big projects to survive, to provide salaries for the 18-man firm."

Thankfully, the newly independent island was in a real need of urban development and renewal. The newly elected government had just started the Sale of Sites scheme by the Urban Renewal Department (URD, the predecessor of today's Urban Redevelopment Authority (URA)). The programme was established to overcome the obstacles to comprehensive urban redevelopment of small land plots under separate private owners. URD assembled small plots into single larger parcels of land, which was then sold by tender to the private sector, accompanied by conditions and concessions to ensure developments would be in line with larger urban planning objectives. This was a major turning point in transforming downtown Singapore from a landscape of shophouses to modern high-rise developments, leveraging on and working with private sector expertise.[4]

At a strategic location in Chinatown was a large open park along Eu Tong Sen Street at the foot of Pearl's Hill. Over time the park evolved into a night market known as People's Park, also referred to as the People's Market, easily the busiest spot in Singapore then. In 1966 it was completely destroyed in a fire. The government saw the importance of this site to Chinatown's urban fabric as well as an opportunity to trigger new growth in the area. In 1967 they put the site up for sale. It was one of the very first Sale of Sites exercises for the URD.

Seow Chuan had lived in Chinatown as a child, so he was very familiar with the area. "I roamed the area as a young boy, so I knew it well. I saw how people moved from one end of People's Park in the middle of Chinatown, to the other end, the Majestic Theatre side. And then from the Majestic Theatre side to Outram. There was a spine, there

---

[4] Urban Redevelopment Authority by Shereen Tay https://www.nlb.gov.sg/main/article-detail?cmsuuid=7a64797c-e86c-44ac-ab2f-6c82a5e213b5.

was already a flow, a system of people moving that the locals were familiar with. That knowledge came in handy when we conceptualised the atrium for the People's Park project later."

Seow Chuan places both arms on the table and rests his weight on them. I get the sense he is going to talk about his first big project. "As luck would have it, Ho Kok Cheong, a glass supplier whom we had collaborated with on previous projects, came to the office one day to ask if we knew of any land for rent or lease," Seow Chuan has a sparkle in his eyes. "We quickly suggested the People's Park Market site and urged him to consider tendering for the land and developing the site with a few investment partners. His shop was on South Bridge Road, so he knew Chinatown quite well. Back then, nobody saw the potential of People's Park except him. He lived there and knew that a lot of the shop owners had money, they had cash. So, as it happened, we received our first big project in the first year of our firm's existence through him. Of course, we did not know then, that the project would have many firsts, it would take on an architectural life of its own. It established Design Partnership as a pioneering force, leading us to many other big projects later."

The People's Park Complex was the beginning of what Prime Minister Lee Kuan Yew called private-sector public-sector participation, through urban planning and urban redevelopment. "Being the first URD project, we knew that the government was more anxious than anyone else for it to be successful; it was the first time the public and private sectors were able to come together and work as one," Seow Chuan beams. "We took it as a chance to do something extraordinary."

It was a great opportunity to make a difference, not just for the firm, but also for Singapore. Since it was the first mall, it had to be a building that could attract and draw Singaporeans from every corner of the island, it had to pay homage to the history of the place, both as a park and as a marketplace.

"I go back to my principle of allowing the site to speak to us, harmonising with the surrounding environment, being true to and understanding the space," Seow Chuan's voice continues to hold steady. Decades may have passed, but we are talking about Design Partnership's first big and most important project, so feelings and facts are still vivid and stark. "I remember, Willy and I would think out loud, and Kheng Soon would try to interpret our ideas three-dimensionally. The three of us talked and sketched frantically all at the same time."

Seow Chuan pauses, seeming to remember something important. "I need to bring you back a little. Many of the firm's design ideas in the late 1960s and 1970s were targeted at the basic social needs and environmental conditions in Singapore. Several key members of Design Partnership were actively involved in the Singapore Planning and Urban Research Group (SPUR), a collective of architects, urban planners, sociologists and economists formed in 1965. William, Kheng Soon and I were part of SPUR, as we were concerned with the urban development of Singapore and how it would affect the common man. In many ways, all three of us were socialist philosophically. We were outspoken on issues, and our group had an uneasy relationship with the newly-elected government. Our intellectual engagement with the issues of the day, and our focus on the people of Singapore fuelled us, and it came to characterise the creative fire of Design Partnership's practice. We became very, very conscious that what we did was for the common man, for the ordinary people of Singapore."

The People's Park Complex reflects this heightened sense of social and environmental awareness. The original People's Park had been a *pasar malam*, an open-air area filled with makeshift stalls where the locals gathered, which was razed to the ground in a fire. The design team now wanted to offer the Chinatown community a place where the locals could congregate again; they were determined not to build an unwelcoming, glitzy new shopping centre that would alienate the average Chinatown dweller.

There were many firsts in the building of People's Park Complex; the financing of the project was also a 'creative' first. The firm was able to get the Urban Renewal Department to agree on the selling-off plan. The building was based on net rentable area, and that gave the architects a lot of possibilities. It was the first mixed-use building: retail, residence and office space. "We had not built it yet, but we had the plan worked out and approved. The next step was selling the plan; we promised to build this, to deliver that, and we managed to work out a system of instalment payments. It was all about cash flow; we needed cash flow to complete the project. If the money came in too slowly, the project could stall, and the government would interfere. So, the project was cash flow driven. At that time, the developers were selling at S$400 per square foot. I magine, if you had a small 200 square foot office, you were talking about S$80,000, a lot of money at the time. The construction cost was in excess of S$10 million. We had to come up with many innovative ideas to keep the budget in check. For example, we recommended no air-conditioning. We worked with the structural engineer YS Lau to come up with the best wall that was cheapest and easiest to build. We devised a system of using precast concrete panels that a single person could carry and install safely from within the building to form the exterior cladding system. In the end, the external walls that went up to 29 floors, the two narrow ends, were built 'from the inside' and we did not need scaffolding to go up the floors." Seow Chuan remembers this with a tinge of nostalgia in his voice. "The building was originally left as raw, unpainted concrete to celebrate materiality and form in the tradition of Frank Lloyd Wright and Le Corbusier. Unfortunately, during the late 1980s, it was painted over.

"When we studied the site conditions and the habitation of Chinatown, we felt a need to insert a civic component to the design that was not in the sales condition: the City Room (atrium). This became the most vital aspect of the success of the building," Seow Chuan recalls the City Room idea with a smile. "The City Room was originally questioned by the developers as it was not considered a revenue-generating space. But because the community-based design was at the heart of the project, we insisted, saying a big building needed a big common space. As the first shopping mall to have an internal multi-storey atrium, the complex spawned imitators throughout the region. Maki visited when the project was completed, and exclaimed, 'We theorised and you people got it built.' I was glad that the 'City Room' served to retain the busy character of Chinatown."

The residential tower block also featured an open-air communal space on every fifth floor where the elevators would stop for the residents to interact. "Because we had to be mindful of the budget, the elevators could not stop on every floor, only every fifth floor. But this allowed the design team the opportunity to create vertical neighbourhoods in five-floor clusters; a kind of 'kampong spirit' was conjured at the lift lobbies, nicknamed the 'sky corridor'. A horizontal striation of floor clusters also gave the building a lighter mass, a break if you like, of the continuous exterior of the tower."

The People Park's Complex was a resounding success. When it was completed in 1972, the complex became a hotspot for the Chinatown community. The modern toilet and bathing facilities were perpetually overused by residents. "Across the road, the people in shophouses, who still used the common bucket system, would come to use the toilets, some of them would bathe in the washrooms. In the evenings, people would gather in the complex's atrium like their own 'living room', away from their cramped sleeping quarters. At 31 storeys, People's Park Complex was one of the tallest buildings constructed in Singapore at the time, and the tallest project completed by Design Partnership. It was a great success because we created a people's space, an urban space where people felt comfortable. This in turn helped the shops and F&B outlets. They were well-received by Singaporeans from all over the island."

At a total site area of one hectare, a building area of 78,500 square metres, and at a total cost of just over S$14 million, People's Park Complex signified an important paradigm shift in the building environment of Singapore's future. "Suddenly, Design Partnership found itself an authority on the building of shopping malls, because we built the first one. With People's Park Complex, we went away learning so much, be it spatial programming, contextual social conditions, creative financing or innovative construction techniques. We pioneered capabilities and systems that put us in a good position for many other major projects."

In a position paper, "Too Young to Die, Giving New Lease of Life to Singapore's Modernist Icons", published by the Singapore Heritage Society in August 2018, Chua Ai Lin looked at three buildings of great historical and architectural significance to Singapore: the Pearl Bank Apartments, People's Park Complex, and Golden Mile Complex. The paper asserted, "Unlike today, where large-scale architectural projects in Singapore often hire foreign corporate professionals for their 'international renown and brand name assurance', Pearl Bank Apartments, People's Park Complex and Golden Mile Complex were

wholly the work of Singaporean talent. These Singapore architects did not merely copy foreign styles but drew on concepts from diverse international sources to 'devise buildings that responded inventively to local conditions.'"[5]

People's Park Complex was internationally hailed as a masterpiece of 1970s experimental architecture, something Seow Chuan still marvels at. "We just wanted to make it happen, for Chinatown, for the people. When it was being built, I remember sitting around the site, making sure it stuck to budget, was on time, that we were working within the rules and regulations. We were doing everything for the first time, and I remember telling myself, at every step of the way, if it was for the greater good, we would stick our necks out, fight for it. Its success gave us many subsequent projects, but for now, I just want to remember it as our maiden voyage, one where thankfully, everything went better than well."

Model shown at Victoria Memorial Hall during an exhibition in 1968 with three Directors of the development company.

[5] *Transformation of the City: The Sale of Site Programmes*. Page 7.

hari raya
aidil-fitri
Bata
Bata
Bata
有限公司
PEOPLE'S SCHOLARSHIP FAIR
FOR COMMUNICATIONS IN AID OF PEOPLE'S SCHOLARSHIP FUND
10.00 A.M. TO 10.00 P.M. OPENING CEREMONY

百貨有限公司
(PTE) LTD.

**"As it reaches its 50th year,
a group of people saw it
for what it should be.
The Golden Mile Complex
is set to emerge again soon,
wearing a conservation crown,
this time, in greater splendour."**

03

The Golden Mile Complex

Launched to Critical Acclaim

Chapter 3

The Golden Mile Complex

Protecting What We Built

The one sure fact of life is, we grow old. Some of us keep fit and stay healthy, others prefer to relax a little more, worry a little less. If we take stock of our lives at middle age, it's a good gauge of how we will continue into old age, unless, of course, we change course midway. What happens to human beings happens to buildings as well, albeit on a bigger and more showy scale. The story of the Golden Mile Complex is the story of a building launched to critical acclaim. Attention then shifted to other buildings and it slowly went into neglect, even disrepute, languishing for decades. As it reaches its 50th year, a group of people saw it for what it should be. The Golden Mile Complex is set to emerge again soon, wearing a conservation crown, this time, in greater splendour.

If you are in an old housing estate, and happen to see a bespectacled photographer organising his shots, the photographer is likely to be Darren Soh. Since 2001, Darren has been a full-time independent photographer, doing a mixture of personal, editorial and commercial work with particular focus on architectural and landscape photography. But the 47-year-old is also known among his peers for photographing old buildings, some of which have already been torn down. In 2018, in a call-for-help move, he held an exhibition, *Before It All Goes, Architecture from Singapore's Early Independence Years.*

"Judging from the people who have come for the exhibition and emails and messages I've been receiving, it appears that many people do care that their memories and childhood spaces are being destroyed in the name of progress," Darren told *The Business Times* on 24 August 2018.

Of particular interest and pain to Darren were some of Singapore's modernist icons, such as Golden Mile Complex and People's Park Complex. These were built by local architects at a time when the country was a newly independent nation finding its footing on the world stage. They reflected the bold spirit of the time, one when the old way of thinking was being discarded, and a brave new way was being forged.

"Unfortunately, many of these shining examples are now either going to be demolished or being put on collective sales, on the road to demolition," he said. "I feel that this will create a state of national amnesia, where we will be missing a huge gap in our built history because we have many conserved pre-war and colonial buildings but only a handful of post-independent buildings have been gazetted."[1]

At about the same time, a group of 12 architects came together to put forth a petition appealing to the URA to gazette Golden Mile Complex and People's Park Complex with conservation status. Like Darren, they were alarmed by the speed at which the wrecking ball would soon hit Pearl Bank Apartments, and that the Golden Mile Complex management corporation strata title (MCST) had garnered more than 80% consensus to proceed with an en bloc sale. "With the gazette, the development model for the new owners will be one of conservation, re-imagination and rejuvenation, rather than the

---

[1] "Yesterday Once More" by Tay Suan Chiang, *The Business Times*, 24 August, 2018.

traumatic process of demolition and new erection," said associate professor of architecture Chang Jiat Hwee.[2]

Completed in 1973, the Golden Mile Complex is both a commercial and a residential property located between Beach Road and Nicoll Highway. Like the People's Park Complex, it was one of the government's urban renewal projects. The complex resembles a giant typewriter when viewed from Nicoll Highway. The stepped-terrace architectural design makes it a colossal edifice, as it gives a panoramic view of the sky and sea, facing the Kallang Basin. The 16-floor complex is about 89 meters tall, accommodating up to 411 shops and 500 parking places. The lower floor contains a retail mall and offices while the upper floors contain the apartments. The building was previously named Woh Hup Complex, the name of the developer. Subsequently Design Partnership suggested naming the building Golden Mile Complex, which was accepted by the developer.

In August 2018, it was announced that the building was going en bloc as 724 owners of 550 units had signed the collective sale agreement — representing 80.83 per cent of the total share value of the development — and the required approval of 80 per cent had been met. With property development in Singapore, money does not just talk, it shouts. Many large and interesting privately held modernist buildings have perished in the name of 'redevelopment and unlocking the value of the site'. Understandably, the announcement caused alarm among conservationists who feared the worst, that the new developer would demolish the building and build a new one in its place.

Aside from the monetary motive, why were the occupants of the complex so eager to sell the building?

The Golden Mile Complex has had a chequered history. When it

---

[2] "Conserve a building, save the planet" by Chang Jiat Hwee, *The Straits Times*, Opinion 12 November 2020.

was completed, it was hailed as a visionary breakthrough, one of the best examples of brutalist designs and the first development in Singapore with an unblocked 'sea view' of the Kallang Basin. Yet today, if you suggest meeting at the Golden Mile Complex, most Singaporeans would be surprised, and a grimace would follow. Younger Singaporeans may not even know where Golden Mile is, having grown up with the glitzy Orchard Road malls and Marina Bay Sands. The complex went from being seen as an icon of national pride to being called a sleazy slum, and now it is being considered part of Singapore's heritage worthy of conservation. Few other developments have had such a long history, with so many ups and downs.

The epochal design of the complex was a source of pride, but how it was managed led to its sunken reputation. Foreign workers who frequented the area were known to get into fights. The building also came to be known as a kind of 'Little Thailand', especially in the 1980s, as many of the Thai foreign construction workers liked to gather there. This led to the emergence of Thai food and beverage outlets, retail shops and also multiple Thai discos. By the 1990s, the complex was attracting undesirable dwellers. Poor maintenance also gave its toilets the dubious reputation of being the filthiest in the country. In 1995, a fire broke out in a canteen, injuring three people. This fire was widely reported in the media, sinking its ragtag reputation even further.

Then in 2006, the situation took a turn for the worse. Nominated MP Ivan Png called Golden Mile a 'vertical slum' and 'national disgrace'. This was what he said in Parliament in March 2006: "The appearance of Golden Mile Complex appals me whenever I drive along Nicoll Highway. It must create a terrible impression on foreign visitors arriving from the airport. How can we be a world-class city in a garden? The Golden Mile Complex is just the most extreme of how a strata-titled property can deteriorate. It illustrates what economists call a 'negative externality'. Each individual owner acts selfishly, adding extensions, zinc sheets, patched floors, glass, all without any regard for other owners and without any regard for national welfare. The result is market failure. Unless we take resolute measures, other strata buildings will go that way."[3]

As complaints and criticisms reached deafening levels, suddenly, calls for its conservation also surged. "A sizable chunk of Singapore's heritage is modernist," said conservation architect Ho Weng Hin. "And modernist heritage still has latent value that can be unlocked." The architect was the founding member of Docomomo Singapore, founded in early 2021 as a local branch of an international group dedicated to promoting and preserving modern architecture. Its website features a list of 100 modern buildings around the city. Some entries are well known and appreciated, like Tiong Bahru Estate and the Asia Insurance Building, or Chinese-American architect IM Pei's OCBC Centre.

However, many are overlooked residential, commercial, industrial and civic structures from the early years of Singapore's independence — buildings such as Golden Mile Complex, whose somewhat grubby appearance belies its roots in the avant-garde architectural movements of the 1960s and early 1970s. "These buildings encapsulate the spirit of the times, we could have been struggling as a backwater, but instead there was a reimagination of what the city and our society could be," says Ho. For the Docomomo Singapore group, the reasons these modernist buildings should be preserved is not just to keep the past alive. "We need to have creative options to reuse buildings, not just for heritage reasons but for social reasons and for environmental reasons as well. We are trying to promote another way of having redevelopment

[3] Golden Mile Complex by Faizah bte Zakaria, Singapore Infopedia.

and regeneration that doesn't involve demolition."[4]

The important word was 'adaptive' reuse.

Koh Seow Chuan is in a reflective mood. He has followed the fate of Golden Mile Complex closely. Developers and architects involved in the future of the complex have been in touch with him. Like the People's Park Complex, how Golden Mile was built still resonates strongly with him. "It was our second big project, following the success of People's Park Complex. We did not want to be just a one hit wonder, so Golden Mile needed to be successful, or, even more successful, given how much we had learnt from People's Park," Seow Chuan looks at me, eyes unblinking. "Modernism emerged in the first decades of the 20th century when architects embraced new building technologies such as reinforced concrete, which allowed us to design things we had never been able to before. If you look at the Tiong Bahru Estate, Singapore's oldest public housing neighbourhood, it was an example of the streamlined modern style. After the war, architects continued to experiment with new approaches, leading to movements like Brutalism, which found beauty in raw, exposed concrete, and Metabolism, a concept hatched in Tokyo that imagined buildings which functioned like living beings. Both these movements found themselves expressed in the Golden Mile Complex, which was designed by us, then, also a pioneering firm," Seow Chuan pauses and takes a sip of water. "The design concept behind both People's Park Complex and Golden Mile Complex share one simple belief: that architecture done properly and done well, can promote social bonding, enrich the human experience and ultimately uplift lives. We got together enlightened developers who were DP clients alongside DP to imagine the right adaptive reuse and

---

4 "Conserving Singapore's Modern" by Low Shi Ping from *d + a* Issue 116 by Design and Architecture.

suggested solutions which were financially viable and doable. We went to government departments with solutions and not just there to ask for handouts, or to conserve a building and make it museum-like. We worked behind the scenes and formulated doable solutions."

Over the years, Seow Chuan has kept a finger on the pulse of the complex. "The complex was originally meant to herald a new era for the Beach Road area, with the authorities intending to have a 'golden mile' of skyscrapers with hotels, shops and luxury apartments. Instead, residents watched as redevelopment efforts took place more aggressively elsewhere, with the rise of icons like Gardens by the Bay and Marina Bay Sands. As a city within a city, it was successful, but it was pretty much on its own at one end of Beach Road. The surrounding areas were not developed as originally planned."

On 22 October 2021, Golden Mile Complex was gazetted for conservation, a year after the government announced its intention to do so. This made it the first modern, large-scale, strata-titled development to be conserved in Singapore. It was a breakthrough for heritage groups championing the conservation of modernist buildings. The move paved the way for other post-independence modernist buildings, which face similar and significant conservation challenges, to be protected.

Seow Chuan looks up. From his eyes, I see joy; what they pioneered isn't just celebrated but considered valuable enough to be conserved, all an important part of Singapore's post-independence story. "The conservation proposal of the URA was accompanied by an incentive package to make development options for the site more attractive to a potential developer. These incentives had been refined over the span of a year, taking into consideration the owners' feedback. The development potential of the site was increased with conservation. The developer will be able to build a new tower block beside the conserved building."

"In a country where land is a limited and expensive commodity, it is inevitable that conserved buildings have to be 'rejuvenated' and adaptively-reused because it would not justify their conservation otherwise," Darren Soh sounds cautiously optimistic. "We live in a country where the land on which these buildings sit becomes more valuable than the buildings themselves over time, so there will always be the attraction of 'cashing out'... We can only trust that the URA will ensure that the new owners allow Golden Mile Complex to be accessible and appreciated by members of the public in the future. There is really no other way if we don't want Golden Mile Complex to be physically erased."

While Darren senses optimism and is cautiously hopeful Golden Mile Complex will eventually be conserved, DP Architects is busily working out solutions to make conservation doable and reaching out to potential clients.

Darren's optimism has allowed him to cautiously hope that other buildings may also be kept away from the demolition path, "Any architecturally significant space or one with strong collective memories of the people, built in the 60s to the 80s, are good candidates," he says hopefully. "People's Park Complex, for being the first large mixed-use project in Asia and one that embodied the Japanese Metabolists' vision of a city in a building. It has also become an icon of Chinatown." The others on his wish list are The Science Centre and various HDB projects built in the 1960s and 1970s.

On 5 May 2022, Golden Mile Complex was sold for S$700 million to a consortium comprising Perennial Holdings, Sino Land, and Far East Organization in a record time: the sale took only 15 days. It marked Singapore's first collective sale of a large strata-titled development as a conserved building. Perennial Holdings has a 50% stake in the joint-venture, while Sino Land and Far East Organization have 25% each. In a statement, the trio said the existing building will be sensitively restored, with special attention paid to retaining its key features and signature terraced profile.

"Perhaps finally, the mile will be paved in gold." Seow Chuan allows a smile. All three components of the consortium are clients of DP Architects!

Wave of Success

Design Partnership, which in 1975 became DP Architects Pte Ltd, is now a design conglomerate and consultancy, and Seow Chuan steals time away from his day to reminisce about the good old days. They weren't just good, they were pioneering and innovative. Design Partnership was literally the first architecture firm to 'nation-build' with the government and developers. They learned, innovated and found ways to be efficient with building cost, were the first to sell off plans, and were responsible for getting the region to look to Singapore for inspiration. With the help of his wife, Seow Chuan has kept the documents, photographs and articles of each building they built like the way he kept his stamps, meticulously comprehensive and in order. "Those were heady days. Getting the design approved was one thing, 'selling' it to the various stakeholders was quite another. But the success of the People's Park Complex made everything easier. It was our passport to the subsequent developments: the Golden Mile Complex, Katong Shopping Centre, Tanglin Shopping Centre. The government had confidence in us, developers sought us out. Our idea was to put the best talent into each project. The firm must have talented people with integrity, honour and honesty who will then be able to take the firm further. That has been our aspiration in any collaboration. If you have a firm honouring just one person, usually the firm dies after this person is gone. But we want a firm that can survive, live and continue the spirit on which the firm was founded. The spirit of the firm was more important than the people."

For the People's Park Complex, Seow Chuan led the team. For the Golden Mile Complex project, "It was total teamwork," he quips. "Chan Sui Him held frequent discussions with Yong Nam Seng, the eldest brother in the developer's team. The way we organised our project at the time, we would have our partners meeting first thing in the morning, every morning. Our first office was at International Building on Orchard Road. We met in the partners' room. When there were confidential matters we would discuss, we had the doors closed. When there were no confidential matters, we had these meetings with the doors opened, anyone could walk in if they wished to join in the meeting or consult us. These mornings were where we would put our heads together to see if there had been leads through our connections."

The two Yong brothers, part of the Singapura Development, were also owners of Woh Hup construction company. "Yong Nam Seng, the eldest brother, was closest to Chan Sui Him. Yong Tet Miaw, the second brother, was closest to me. Both Sui Him and I spent a lot of time with the developer on the project. The Yong brothers thought it was a project with great potential. The site was the end of the Beach Road ribbon, there was an Orchard Road corridor, there was also a Beach Road corridor. We were so enthusiastic about the site that we began to see the site not by itself, but more in the context of the immediate surrounding area. We saw the possibility of a ribbon forming along from this site to Raffles Hotel. We then drew up a whole masterplan for the Golden Mile, how we could create a continuity of buildings, from one building to another without being exposed to the tropical elements. Buildings that were linked, a community of buildings where you could go from one end to the other in any weather condition. Later on, we turned this masterplan into a publication, called *A Tropical City of the Future*, with Golden Mile at the end of the ribbon. The beginning of the ribbon was where the war monument was. It was called Golden Mile because it was supposed to be a golden development for a mile."

The inspiration for the design is something I am most intrigued by. I was told the idea for the design was hatched in the late 1960s while they were all part of SPUR. So, how did the unusual shape come about? "In front of Golden Mile was Kallang Bay. We needed to respond to the water, we didn't think a high-rise box building would be in sympathy with that kind of environment in front of the Kallang Bay. We wanted the building to take its form by responding to the water, so that was why we sloped the building. And because the contractor was also the developer, they took up the challenge of building it like a wave. So, the shape of the building was like a wave or the continuation of a wave."

This reference to a wave is not mentioned in any literature I have read; I cannot contain my fascination. Was the inspiration similar to the famous Japanese wave? "Think of it moving up," he says, his voice suddenly tense with excitement. "The design needed to be 'softer', if I may use the word, it could not be a wall or glass wall. The balconies were big and they came together to create the effect. We were thinking, living in the tropics, we wanted the line between the outdoor and indoor blurred. The balconies were luxurious, big enough to hold up to 20 people. From breakfast, lunch, to dinner and evening drinks, the space was designed for camaraderie, it was luxurious community living where you could say hi to your neighbours by just reaching and looking out."

A continuation of a wave, the balconies encouraging community living. A bold move away, yet also a continuation of the People's Park Complex, where getting people together was the focus. Golden Mile was the first major, post-independent riverfront luxury property in Singapore. Like People's Park, the building form responded to the site. In terms of architecture, it was unique and more iconic than People's Park Complex because of the site, and the way it was built. And this time, the developer and contractor were in on the game, they saw themselves very much a part of the architectural team. "If we did not have a good contractor, we might have had many accidents on the site because of the design." Seow Chuan's eyes dart to the right, thinking. "The success of Golden Mile Complex was due to teamwork. And it was a larger team. The consultants, Ove Arup group, were crucial for this project. Everything was aligned, this alignment was the one thing that could not be sacrificed or compromised upon particularly for a project like this. Because of the sloping form, we needed all talented hands on-deck. I must mention the developers here. The Yongs trusted the creative team, appreciated the design. They allowed the architects to be bold and brave, even if it cost more. They had faith that in the end, it was money well spent. They had foresight, they invested in these peoples' creativity, believing they would make money eventually. So, they didn't put obstacles in front of the creative team. The best developers are those who leave the architects alone to create, to innovate. Leave everyone, every professional, to deliver to the best of their talent and ability."

For People's Park Complex, the atrium energised the entire project, the atrium in the Golden Mile project was designed as an enclosed linear street that could be extended to connect to the next adjacent building. "The sloping facade was the most characteristic feature of Golden Mile, it was done at some increased cost, and that needed to be managed," Seow Chuan's mind is now back on the construction site, in the early 1970s. "We were in good hands, we engaged the Ove Arup group, the civil structural engineering firm with the right experience. The slope had to be anchored by the columns and the slabs. So, it was a different form of construction structurally. It had to be sequenced right for the columns and the floor to go up. That was the most complicated. Also because of the slope, we had to keep everything else simple. No cosmetics to contain the cost. The surface, like People's Park, was raw, and for a long time we did not have to do anything to the surface."

Golden Mile was a more difficult project to build, and because it was more difficult, Design Partnership formed a team to handle it specifically and that worked out much better. It was a tougher project in terms of management. "For People's Park, the balancing of the budget was the most important. We had to create a way of building the walls from the inside without having scaffolding. People's Park did not have a success to depend and rest on. Golden Mile had the benefit of confidence and success created by its predecessor. Here, the developer was very keen to see it as a success story and to use it for other buildings, taking them to the next level. They were keen to see it as a milestone project. The Yong brothers were comfortable with me and Chan Sui Him, they saw us as people who could see different points of view. We could disagree and tell them why. And we could put the disagreements to rest and move on or come to an agreement."

When it was completed, it cost 50% more than People's Park Complex, but everyone, including the media, saw it as a bigger success. It was hailed as an architectural wonder, an icon, one of the finest examples of post-war modernist architecture. "We were glad it was an original design inspired from the ground, the site and its surroundings, not by any other building." He rests both his hands on the table now. "In the intermittent years, it went through a rough patch. When it is restored, it will be a gem again, an old jewel with an interesting past."

GOLDEN MILE
SHOPPING
CENTRE

"Today, Esplanade with its twin domes has grown to be a symbol and part of Singapore's consciousness. Our unique architecture has become a familiar landmark and how Singaporeans identify home. Drawing on the fond memories of some and promise for others of new possibilities."

Lee Tzu Yang

04

Esplanade – Theatres on the Bay

From left to right: Koh Seow Chuan, Michael Wilford and Vikas M Gore.

Chapter 4

Esplanade – Theatres on the Bay

Rough Seas

There was high drama, indeterminate controversies, and everyone had a view. It would take more than a decade to complete; few public projects had a rougher and messier ride. But when it was done, everyone wanted a piece of it. The media went to town, and everyone had a special name for it: from the eyes of a fly to the king of fruits, the beloved durian. Accolades poured in from all corners of the world and it won prestigious architectural awards. Its critics went into hiding, completely silenced.

"You can say it is a Cinderella story, it ended well, but if you had to live through the decade…" Seow Chuan pauses. "Only those close to me knew how much I suffered. It was easily the most controversial episode of my entire life."

This morning Seow Chuan is full of energy because we are talking about the defining project of his architectural career. The People's Park Complex was the start, the Golden Mile Complex an affirmation that the start was no fluke. This, Esplanade — Theatres on the Bay, would be the prize. Wen Gin has just made me a cup of thick black coffee. A few sips and my senses are sharp and alive. I want to know everything there is to know about the Esplanade, from the very start, everything.

"It was a bold vision, you need to understand, we were sitting on the edge of a new millennium," Seow Chuan's calm voice is reflective. "The design team wanted to leave the last century behind, we saw this as a beacon for a new start in a brand-new era. It would have no precedent. We knew that those in the know would want us to reference performing arts centres like the Sydney Opera House, or perhaps buildings like the Guggenheim Museum. But we were adamant, we wanted a performance centre for the arts like no other. It would embody a new Singapore, the spirit of a people who had found a footing in the global world. A Singapore that had taken care of life's basics, like housing and schooling, and had now become a centre of finance. Unlikely as it might have seemed, it was ready to be a centre for the arts. Built for a globalised and connected Singapore, it had to push the limits of new technologies coming on stream at ever increasing pace. This building could not be a mere copy or variation of the many multi-venue centres built in the previous fifty years. It was to be the first of a new century."

The idea of a new arts centre for Singapore had been discussed as early as 1984. Then 24-year-old architecture student Mark Chin was quoted in the *Straits Times* as saying, "... it should cater to both large-scale performances and small groups... People should walk by and experience its presence." In 1987, the first function brief was drawn up by the government, and two years later, the government accepted recommendations made by the Advisory Council on Culture and the Arts to build a multi-venue arts centre. A Steering Committee was set up in 1990, chaired by then Deputy Prime Minister Ong Teng Chong.

"The government said we needed a cluster of performing venues. The Victoria Theatre and Concert Hall were good venues, but they would not be big enough for big performances, and they were colonial leftovers. There was the Substation, small, again not quite good enough. Tan Chin Nam, a high-flying civil servant, advocated the idea of a cultural renaissance through his paper. 'A Renaissance Nation in the Knowledge Age'." Seow Chuan opens a file of newspaper cuttings and documents. "To quote him, 'As Singapore matures into an advanced economy, art should no longer be viewed as a luxury, but a strategic investment tool that contributes towards both the economic competitiveness and social well-being of our nation.'[1] All these pointed to how important this new performing centre for the arts would be. I started to prepare myself and DP Architects for it; I had my eye on the project way before anyone else. I was convinced that it would be the most important architectural structure post-independence."

Unlike People's Park and Golden Mile Complex, a performing arts centre was on a different scale, for the government was acutely aware that it would attract interest internationally. Seow Chuan soon realised what he and DP Architects had done might not be enough to convince the government that they were suitable for the job. "To them, we must always learn from the past, go out and see the best examples of what the outside world can offer us. If anything happened, we could always say we learnt and we followed from the best examples of the world. So, it became clear that teaming up with foreign architects was going to be important."

In 1988, Seow Chuan had been working on Temasek Polytechnic, the first polytechnic in Singapore, collaborating with James Stirling, Michael Wilford & Associates. He travelled to London often where the work was being planned and conceptualised. "I always said we conceptualised together. I have the privilege and standing to say we do

[1] Tan Chin Nam — Esplanade Offstage https://www.esplanade.com/offstage/arts/tan-chin-nam.

it as equals. A Westerner may have more experience, and I have less, but I know how to get it done in Singapore. And I know what Singapore needs. Being multicultural, multi-religious, certain things are ingrained in us."

To have previously built a performing arts centre was one of the conditions for the shortlist during the pre-qualification exercise to appoint architects for the project. In Singapore, only Alfred Wong & Partners would remotely qualify; they had built the National Theatre at Fort Canning Park, which had subsequently been pulled down. So, the government made it abundantly clear local architects would need to team up with foreigners. James Stirling, Michael Wilford & Associates had built the Performing Arts Centre at Cornell University between 1983 to 1988. When James Stirling passed away in 1992, Michael Wilford & Partners continued the tradition of specialising in building performing arts centres, art galleries and museums, including The Lowry Performing and Visual Arts Centre in Salford, England.[2]

"When the government asked for submissions for pre-qualification in 1991, I had a four-year head start working with a qualified foreign firm," Seow Chuan leans back, folding his arms. "When Michael Wilford was in Singapore, the two of us would end the day in Marco Polo, the hotel designed by Alfred Wong where Michael stayed in. In there, I remember this huge triptych batik artwork by Seah Kim Joo near the bar. Huge, as big as the wall. The scene was a multicultural Singapore, people in various attire, eating hawker food. I remember the setting because I remember what Michael said to me. 'My firm has only 18 people, you have 180,' he said. 'You are capable of doing all this having done People's Park, Golden Mile, and most recently Marina Square.' I

---

[2] James Stirling had no input in the design of the Esplanade.

told him my government didn't think so. It was ironic and somewhat sad that a foreigner who had worked with me on the Temasek Polytechnic project had more faith in me. But I was also realistic, if collaboration with a foreign firm was the pre-requisite, so be it."

48 teams responded to the pre-qualification exercise. Seow Chuan would sit with Michael at Boat Quay, the mouth of the Singapore River, looking at the reclaimed land where the arts centre had been planned to be, mulling over their chances. Three advisory groups were set up, Users' Advisory Group, Aesthetics Advisory Group and Commercial Advisory Group. In August 1992, it was announced that DP Architects Singapore and Stirling Wilford Associates UK had been shortlisted, "We had made the final shortlist of four. DP Architects was the biggest architecture firm then, and we were determined to get the job. Of the 48 teams, we had fielded three teams and when it went down to the last four, two of them were from DP Architects. So, we stood a 50/50 chance."

Choosing the Chef, Not the Dish

The year was 1992. Seow Chuan holds the distinction of being the first Singaporean invited to sign the British Philatelic Federation's Roll of Distinguished Philatelists in Newcastle. It was a rare honour, and Seow Chuan decided to attend with his wife. "It had been hectic, now that we knew we were in the last four, I thought it was a perfect time to take a break with my wife. After Newcastle, we would go on a short holiday."

Wen Gin leans forward calmly. "There was no holiday."

"The government realised it was too complex a project for the right design to emerge after only a few months," Seow Chuan says with a slight grin. "So, the government asked for a public presentation by the Singaporean architects, not their foreign counterparts. We later learned that the government was more interested in selecting a team, not the design. By allowing the Singaporean architects to do a public presentation, the government could decide which local architecture firm knew the situation best. The design could always be refined but if they chose the wrong team, the project would be crippled from the start. So, they were choosing the chef, not the dish."

Wen Gin looks at my empty cup. "I'll get you more coffee," she says. Walking towards the kitchen, she turns back and smiles. "The trip was cut short. On the plane back, he did not talk to anyone, he was busy sketching for the presentation."

Seow Chuan knew the presentation could not be merely architectural. It needed to show DP Architects' understanding of why a cultural centre was important to Singapore. By the 1990s, Singapore had reached the critical middle point of its journey as a nation, and a performing arts centre would be a symbol of this maturity, a crucial cultural jigsaw to complete the nation-building exercise.

"I decided to make a presentation that encompassed nation-building." He folds his arm and sits back. "I said we were at a very important phase of nation-building, 30 years after independence. It was the middle period of our nation-building. We had to get it right. It had to be an arts centre that resonated with the people. The building had to come right from the hearts of Singaporeans, it needed to reflect the spirit of how Singapore was going to survive." He turns and looks me in the eye. "Everyone else was just focused on how the building would look, how to come up with a design that wowed. For me, the correct messaging was more important, that now was the right time to allow the flowering of the arts in Singapore, the coming of age, the maturing of Singapore. Before, nation-building was brick and mortar, the hard requirements like political stability, defence, a roof over our heads. It was now time to look at the softer needs, a performing arts centre would be that important symbol. But this symbol needed to tie back to what Singapore was about, our multi-racialism. We still needed to be one nation, one people. My theme was the flowering of the arts in Singapore for everyone, the next level of nation building."

Instead of talking about the look of the project, he focused on what the building needed to be about. For example, the building needed to be friendly to its surroundings. Unlike western performing art centres which were normally in the middle of the city with roads on all sides, Singapore's performing arts centre would be in the midst of historically significant sites like Fort Canning Park and the Padang. The roofscape of the Esplanade must be pleasing to the eye when viewed from the tall buildings around it. Its scale must also be in sympathy with existing structures in the immediate vicinity — the Civilian Memorial, the Supreme Court and City Hall across the Padang. Therefore, a building on the scale of the Sydney Opera House which looked spectacular at the entrance to the Sydney Harbour would be inappropriate on the Esplanade site. "It is not a big piece of land, and it has an unusual shape, triangular with three fronts and no back. So, how do we create a back to the servicing area? We thought this through, and decided to bring the service area into the basement. So, there is no service road. We were able to create an image, above ground, of a building that rose from the ground. Everything about the site was thought through. I used the imagery of a lotus, which is one of the hardiest flowers. With large, bold, luxuriant leaves standing high above the water, the lotus flower is sturdy and well anchored. Although the flower looks delicate, it is resilient and flowers even in the mud. It is always there, weathering the tropical sun and rain."

This public presentation was well covered in the media; the *Straits*

Times gave many pages to images of the models the four local architects presented. Everyone was caught up with the visuals of what was presented, few cared about the rationale for the designs or which architecture firm would be the best to see this important project through.

"It became a public debate in the media, and it went on for a long time," Seow Chuan shakes his head slowly. "Everyone had a view, from the general public to prominent public figures, students of architecture to professional architects, those who made it to the last 48 and those who didn't. Everyone said the design needed to be unique, but when asked what they meant by unique, most had no answer. Some thought foreigners should be excluded in something this important to the national identity. Too boxy, too squarish, not enough thought given to national symbols, on and on. They even wanted the last four teams to be dumped and for the competition to start anew. They forgot, or did not want to remember, the long journey the country had gone through to get to that point."

Seow Chuan takes a sip of water, tips his head back and smiles. "The Singapore Institute of Architects, SIA, wrote a 'Resolution' to their council members," he smiles again and opens his file to a document dated 21 September 1992. "Let me read from the document, 'The Singapore Institute of Architects has always advocated that for nationally important projects, an open architectural competition is the best way to obtain outstanding architectural designs... SIA is disappointed at the extremely short shortlist and the lack of public knowledge on what criteria the shortlist was based... SIA is deeply concerned at the quality of the four design concepts presented to-date and in particular the apparent lack of originality in some of the designs... SIA is interested in participating and contributing to a successful and worthy final design for the Singapore Arts Centre (SAC). Therefore, the council is charged to prepare a proposal on how such participation and contribution by SIA can be made, including a review of the brief, as it affects the local and regional arts. SIA feels that the SAC design/architect selection processes should be reopened as an open architectural competition.'"

In response, Robert Iau, the Executive Chairman of the SAC, clarified in the newspapers that there was a fundamental misconception among members of the public. SAC was not choosing a design; they were choosing a winning architectural team to do the design. 'The models they have presented are preliminary concepts used to explain their approach and philosophy. Only after we have chosen the architectural team will the actual design process begin. The selected architectural team will have more than a year to design the SAC.'"

On the Brink

On 21 December 1992, it was announced at a press conference that DP Architects would be the local architecture firm to design the Singapore Arts Centre in collaboration with United Kingdom-based James Stirling, Michael Wilford & Associates. Robert Iau stressed that the new centre "will not be one in a long series of Western-inspired arts centres which have been developed. Instead, it will be the first of many great Asian arts centres expected to be built in the years to come."

Robert Iau also gave the reasons why the team won; they did so "because of their flexibility, creativity and good working relationship... This team has an open mind, they are flexible and highly creative in their suggestions and solutions. We need to have a team which is able to interact and respond to the unique situation in Singapore."

At the press conference, Seow Chuan acknowledged that the project was very important for Singapore, and that the team "will come up with a unique solution for it." Michael Wilford added, "Both partners will enjoy an equal role. Both will bring their unique strengths and experience to the project… We're very aware of the multi-ethnic and cultural background of Singapore, part of the challenge is to fuse the performing cultures in one building, which will make it a very unique one."[3]

The next phase would be the design itself. All three, Robert Iau, Seow Chuan and Michael Wilford, used the word "unique". The dictionary defines unique as "being the only one of its kind; unlike anything else". So, expectations were set high. Like what Seow Chuan said earlier, everyone wanted the design to be unique, yet no one knew or had in mind what that uniqueness was. Robert Iau continued, "We have a totally open mind. Our intention is to fuse different cultures in one building… We want this project to be as participatory as possible with the public. After all, it is their Arts Centre."[4]

Singapore Arts Centre would be built on a six-hectare site in Marina Bay. It would house a concert hall, a lyric theatre, a theatre for dance and drama, an adaptable theatre and a small studio. At the end of 1992 the design for the centre did not exist yet. Everyone knew it had to be unique, one of its kind, unlike anything else. This uniqueness had to include elements from the East and the West, a good balance between the traditional and the modern, and it had to convey the multi-cultural character of Singapore, the city's position as a hub and its desire to be a tropical city of excellence. Finally, the design had to be one that would be an inspiration for the people of Singapore. A tall order.

The Singapore Arts Centre, like most performing arts centres in the world, had set itself up for a long, protracted and noisy design

---

3 *The Straits Times*, December 22, 1992.

4 Ibid.

controversy. Everyone was passionate, and felt its importance and significance. Yet at that time, few could put a finger on, or could see in their minds, what it was they truly wished or wanted the centre to be. It was akin to saying, "I don't know what it should be, it just needs to be great on all levels."

Seow Chuan stands, stretching his arms outwards. "We were ready." He sits, now composed. "With Michael Wilford and their considerable experience, I was confident. The design would reveal itself; we just needed to do as much research as we had time for and allow the site to speak to us. We avoided loud rhetoric, theorization and the temptations to make large statements and impose preconceived forms."

Talking about the design, as a national project, the relationship of the site to the Padang and the Civic District beyond it had to be acknowledged. "A ceremonial entrance for state occasions was important, and this was placed facing the Padang. In this way, the arts centre would be linked to the family of important civic buildings just beyond the green space." He pauses, continues, "On its other flank stood the high-rise commercial developments of Marina Square. In order not to block the view of Marina Bay and the city beyond, the scale of the Esplanade had to be appropriate. If the new building was to speak to the rest of the surrounding buildings in a civilised and friendly way, its height needed to 'allow' and compliment, not obstruct. In other words, it would not be a tall building."

At every turn, it was clear the architectural community and the public were impatient. They wanted to see the design of the SAC. The design team refused to be rushed, it took its time, approaching the building with an attitude of curiosity but with no preconceived idea of form. Over time, two distinctive shapes emerged. These were the Concert Hall and Theatre. The former was slightly larger because of its

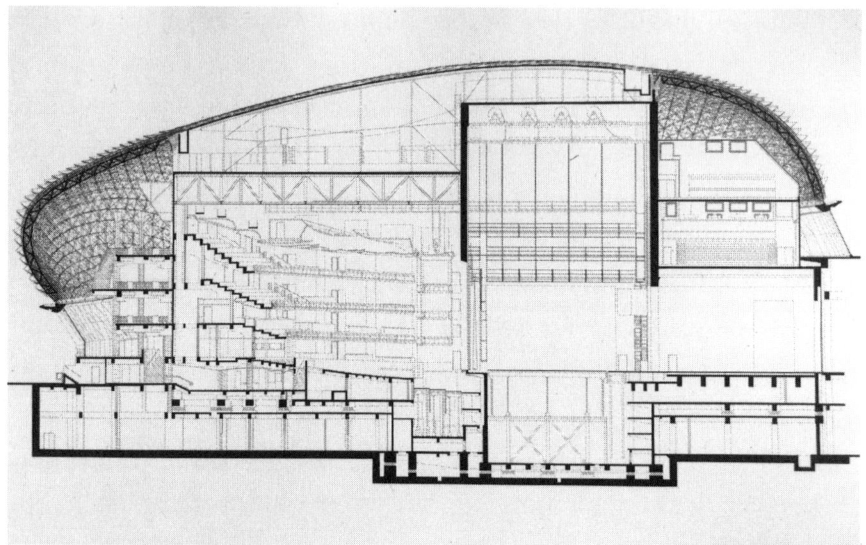

Architectural section through Theatre.

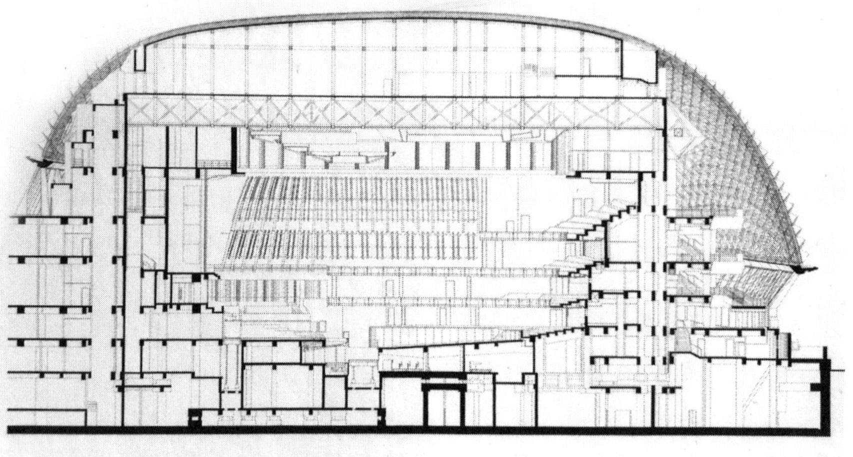

Architectural section through Concert Hall.

acoustic chambers, which occupied almost as much space as the Hall itself. As the largest masses of the project, they dominated the development from every aspect. Each was allowed to reveal and express its function and purpose. It would have been a compromise of their integrity to take the easy option of forcing the shapes into a matching pair, or to contain them in a superimposed shell. No such attempt was made. They were left to stand intact, their complex geometry belying the sleek curves, honest in interpreting their required forms.[5]

From the onset, one of the key briefs for the project was to keep it 'friendly'; it was a people's arts centre. The triangular site was unique in having no backs. It was all fronts, facing the Padang, facing the Marina Square, and facing the water. It offered a distinct opportunity for openness, and a seamless transition between exterior and interior spaces, to reinforce the idea that it was a public space, that it belonged to everyone. Optimising the benefits of having fronts on all sides, the project was conceived as being porous and transparent. The only real walls enclosed the theatre and concert hall to provide controlled conditions for performances. The foyers were wrapped around the halls. Glass was extensively used so that people in the foyers could look out and relate to the exterior, while people outside or driving along the roads would be able to look in, and again feel that this building belonged to them.

The design process inside the structure went smoothly; the public and architectural community left the look of the performing spaces and acoustic details to the professionals. Most Singaporeans were only interested and wanted to have a say in the 'look' of the exterior. In March 1994, the schematic design was completed. In July, models of the art centre were unveiled in a public exhibition, *Taking Shape*. Visitors

---

[5] "The Geometrical Processing of Free-formed Envelopes for The Esplanade Theatres in Singapore" by Jaime Sánchez-Alvarez, MERO GMBH & Co. KG, D -97064 Würzburg, Germany.

could 'walk around' the five venues in virtual reality. The name of the new arts centre, 'Esplanade — Theatres on the Bay', was officially announced by BG George Yeo. Unfortunately, the occasion also allowed for a fresh wave of critical media attention and public criticism.

"Much of the criticism centred on the form or the lack of form of the two big halls." Seow Chuan looks down. "It was in fact a misunderstanding of the schematic model. The purpose of the model and the public presentation was to show the main volumes and their juxtaposition, the external spaces created and their locations in relation to the site. The insides and the acoustics of the five halls had already been designed in some detail. In contrast, the outsides had not yet been designed, therefore they still looked like 'blobs', unfinished. They were sculpture blocks waiting to be sculpted, if you like. The purpose of the public presentation was to get feedback on the master plan, then make adjustments before the architects began work on the detailed design of the external aspects, especially the 'skin'. The 'skin' must keep out the weather, rain and heat, allow views of the sea, the Padang and the Civilian War Memorial, be easy to build and maintain, and look splendid. Many ideas were being explored but no decision had yet been taken on any of them."

This misunderstanding led to louder and louder public criticism, much of which appeared in the local media. It was also clear that the government was taking notice of public sentiments; after all, this was a big government project costing hundreds of millions, touted as a people's arts centre. The minister in the middle of the controversy was the then Minister of Information, Communications and the Arts (MICA), BG George Yeo.

Seow Chuan casts his mind back to a presentation they had to make to the Cabinet. "In 1995, a presentation to the Cabinet ministers on the Esplanade schematic design was requested," he begins. "I was surprised that Minister BG George Yeo had agreed to the presentation date knowing that he would be away in Brunei. Initially, I thought this would be a good opportunity to explain and clarify to the Cabinet ministers what The Esplanade would be, and could be. DP Architects made a 30-minute presentation on the schematic design. Unfortunately, the Cabinet ministers did not appear to appreciate the schematic design. The architects were still working closely with the client, the Singapore Arts Centre Company and the project manager, the Public Works Department and the various specialist consultants on the detailed design: such as the external cladding and the interior design for the Theatres and Concert Hall. We were truly like the chef in the middle of preparing the dish. During the presentation, a Cabinet minister expressed real concern whether The Esplanade could end up as a 'white elephant' and whether Singapore should be spending such a large sum of money on an Arts Centre."

Following the presentation, the government announced that The Esplanade would be funded by the Tote Board and that the development would be in two phases — Theatres and Concert Hall being part of Phase One, and the rest of the performance venues being part of Phase Two.

In June 1995, Michael Wilfred & Partners decided to retire their involvement in the project as they felt DP Architects could continue the project without their firm's involvement. Their retirement was accepted by the Singapore Arts Centre Company and DP Architects continued as the project architect to develop the detailed design and oversee the project to its completion in October 2002.

The Durians

"Let's talk about what gives The Esplanade its Singaporean name, the Durians." Seow Chuan's face literally lights up from within, like a lantern. By now, the architects knew they were working with two huge glass structures. With so much glass, light and heat mechanisms were critical in order to cope with Singapore's tropical climate. The modest height of the development also meant the top of the domed structures would be in full view of the neighbouring high-rise windows. "The solution was to throw a canopy over the whole development," Seow Chuan bends forward, physically preparing himself to talk about the most visible part of the design, the spikes. "Flexibility was a primary requirement, given the complex geometric forms that required cladding. The ability to vary the amount of light admitted was another important element, given the variation in heat and light emanating from the sun. Here we were inspired by nature."

The design team travelled the region to get inspiration for the design; mainly Bali, parts of Thailand and Malaysia. Apart from being informed by Southeast Asian architecture, it was tropical nature which gave them the most clues to the design. "We needed to look out, and the outside needed to look in," he smiles. "So, glass was important. The structures needed to be transparent. But how do we deal with the heat of the sun? I thought of the lotus in the pond, how it needed the sun, yet needed to be protected from it. I further thought about the giant Angsana tree near the Satay Club before the reclamation, the many leaves that gave shade. When I discussed these references with Michael Wilford, he was inspired and impressed. We travelled more and opened our eyes to nature and what it could tell us. Tropical nature became the feasible beginning of the conceptual design. But what we gathered were mere fragments, individual pieces; we needed the dots to be connected to form the master design."

By 1994, the design had evolved to a critical stage and both DP Architects and Michael Wilford's team felt that the cladding of the two remaining venues would become one of the most prominent features of the project. "It had reached a point when it was not just architecture but we also needed the precision of mathematics and science. We needed specialist consultants." Seow Chuan picks up a stack of photostat documents ring-bound together, titled 'SMP ATELIER ONE, ATELIER TEN'. "It was agreed that a specialist consultant of repute should be brought in to assist in the design of the cladding. London-based design engineers Atelier One and environment engineers Atelier Ten were appointed to work with the architects. They had been recommended by Michael Wilford and were told that the idea behind the design was nature-inspired, that they should continue with this vision of the cladding as something that should feel organic and natural. Joint work on the cladding system began in early 1995."

The eventual design was a modular system of shades, which could be installed on a steel frame. The shading panels were made of aluminium, which satisfied the requirements of lightness and durability. The modular frame could be prefabricated for assembly on site, which was a distinct advantage. This was a unique system designed specifically for the arts centre. It allowed for each shading panel or leaf to be individually calibrated for its position relative to the sun's path. Each leaf could be angled for maximum light exposure, or completely closed and overlapping, like the leaves of a tree or scales on a fish. As a further refinement, they could overlap in different directions, as bird's feathers overlap in different orientations, depending on the amount of movement they have to accommodate.

"The leaves were supposed to move with the sunlight, according to the direction of the sun. But the project did not have the budget for it. Eventually the leaves were fixed, so a careful study of the various angles of the sun was conducted. A high-end German contractor was used for the bending of the leaves in various directions. This had to be done with mathematical precision. Some people thought we invested too much time and money into this. But we remembered the original brief, and what we promised. It needed to be unique. We did not want the surface to shut totally, but to have light filtering through, creating drama on the foyer floors and on the walls of the theatre so that there was life. We did not want a place totally dependent on artificial light. A performance building must convey the spirit of performing, even before you enter the hall. The moment you see it, you already start to soak in the experience of performance."

The acoustics of the Esplanade rested on the shoulders of then 78-year-old master acoustician Russell Johnson, and his company, Artec Consultants, based in New York. They had planned and designed the acoustics for more than 10 performing arts buildings worldwide by then. Artec devised a system using design features that were similar to the excellent acoustics of the early 20th-century concert halls. To achieve this, the walls of the Esplanade's Concert Hall were padded with 600 pieces of rubber, and its theatre, 800 pieces. Intermeshed with steel plates, the rubber served to insulate the hall from its surroundings. A 50 mm acoustic gap was also created to separate the hall from the rest of the building. In addition, an acoustic canopy, which was a large sound reflector, ensured a clearer sound. The halls were also fitted with reverberation chambers comprising 84 doors and sound-absorbing curtains. The function was to vary the volume to suit the needs of different performances. This way, both Eastern instruments like the *gamelan* from Indonesia and orchestra or choral performances from the West would sound equally good. Mr Johnson told the Singaporean media, "My vision for the Esplanade is to give audiences a social outing they will never forget."[6]

Even while the design was being finalised, and indeed, way into construction, criticisms from professionals and the public continued. There were incessant and direct comparisons made to the Sydney Opera House, and the verdict was always the same, that the Esplanade fell short, that it would be a very public failure. Public opinion only started to change slowly towards the end of the construction, when the distinctive cladding took shape, and it became clear that the visuals of Esplanade — Theatres on the Bay would create an impact, it would be a striking and distinctive edifice, one that would transform the Singapore's cityscape. The spiky finish caught the imagination of the public, and way before it was officially launched, Singaporeans had started to call it by what it looked like to them: an inverted bra, then *sea hum* (cockles), papaya and finally the durians. These were everyday playful images the general public knew and were fond of. So even before the Esplanade opened its doors to the public, it had crept into their fascination, becoming a people's centre as it had set out to be.

"Before it was completed, Fumihiko Maki asked me to walk him through the place. Even Marina Bay Sands architect Moshe Safdie came to me for a tour as the 'leaves' were coming up when the structure was close to completion. It caught the attention of the world because of the controversy and how surprised they were when they saw what it was turning out to be."

---

[6] "Man behind the sound" by Camilla Chiam. *The Straits Times Life!* August 10, 2002.

Esplanade — Theatres on the Bay opened in October 2002, at a cost of S$600 million. "Since gaining independence in 1965, Singapore has become an economic dynamo," wrote the international architecture magazine ArchNewsNow.com. "And a local truism says there are five 'Cs' to happiness: car, cash, condo, credit card, and country club. The Esplanade is the government's impressive step to add a sixth 'C' — culture — to the mix."[7] This was just one example of many good reviews the new art centre garnered following its opening. Three years later, it received the prestigious Royal Institute of British Architects (RIBA) Worldwide Design Award. In 2006, it was selected as the Design of the Year for the inaugural President's Design Award Singapore.

Jury Citation:

The Esplanade Theatre rises up to the urban design challenge of creating a 360-degree building with no true rear or backyard, fully addressing the waterfront and the surrounding developments in the Marina Bay area and the Civic District. The Jury commends the Esplanade's exemplary provision of public spaces to encourage vibrant activities, technical dexterity and its seamless transition from the outside to inside. With its distinctive roof, the Esplanade Theatres emerges from the foreground of Marina Bay as a contemporary icon, anchoring the northwest corner of the waterfront with a sweeping view of the bay. It has also placed a high value on achieving superb acoustic performance. The Esplanade Theatres have grown to become a talking point for Singaporeans and visitors alike and is one of the most recognisable icons representing Singapore.

---

[7] Esplanade — Theatres on the Bay by Michael Wilford & Partners; DP Architects, by Kristen Richards, 16 January 2003 http://www.archnewsnow.com/features/Feature101.htm

In the end, Esplanade — Theatres on the Bay became a good example of teamwork in architecture. "DP Architects alone could not have done it," Seow Chuan's face is relaxed, now that he has come to the end of the Esplanade story, a long story. "It needed foreign participation for Singapore did not have the relevant knowledge then. As it was coming up, people could see it was going to be an outstanding edifice. It was going to be different. We wanted it to be unique, and as it took form, we knew it was — an original gem that glittered in the day and glowed at night. We allowed that uniqueness to unravel as we went along. When it was all done the many critics were quiet."

CONRAD
SAMSUNG

"The pride, the respect and energy in the room attest to the success of Seow Chuan's formula that sometimes you may have to give way if you wish to win the big prize. This is a valuable lesson, that few great men in the world know."

Mrs Pamelia Lee

On DP Architects' 50th Anniversary

05

Change and Consolidation by Design

Chapter 5

Change and Consolidation by Design

Design Partnership to DP Architects

Two decades before Esplanade — Theatres on the Bay, the firm went through seminal and significant changes. The transition from Design Partnership to DP Architects Pte Ltd in 1975 signalled an important shift for the firm. The practice had started small, with 15 employees in 1967. By 1975 it had grown into a firm of over 60 staff. DP Architects was known for large-scale, noteworthy projects throughout the country and increasingly, the region. With the transition to larger, more complicated projects, the practice needed to expand its manpower to meet the demands of multi-projects running at different stages. In 1975, Tay Kheng Soon left to form his own firm, Akitek Tenggara.

"The first period was 1967 to 1975. The period after that, from 1975 onwards, was change and consolidation by design," says Seow Chuan. "Teamwork and collaboration are the foundation of a partnership. When Design Partnership became DP Architects Pte Ltd, the spirit of teamwork and collaboration was enhanced. DP took an institutional form but retained the spirit of the partnership, like old wine in a new bottle. Real change began in late 1981, continuing with the original spirit of the early partnership."

The transition from a partnership to a private company signalled a shift in the way the partners wanted to run the practice. By adopting the structure of a privately held company, the partners would now form a board of directors who held shares of the company. That meant that the continuation of the practice did not rely on the original founding partners. DP Architects would exist as an entity on its own. Succession planning for the future of DP Architects was in place to ensure progress through growth in the hands of the next generation of leadership. Apart from the organisational benefits, the transition also brought about a more secure and stable business model. This dedication to self-renewal and the prioritisation of the firm's collective ability over any individual member is a cornerstone of the practice's beliefs to this day.

"When we became DP Architects, we wanted to form a firm that would survive us after we're gone." Seow Chuan's voice is now resolute and focused. "I took a special interest in firms that have survived over 100 years. We can learn from history, history will let us better understand the present, and we will probably be able to visualise and position ourselves into the future. Rodyk & Davidson, R&D, is Singapore's oldest law firm; it has survived for more than a century. Studying them, I learned three things from R&D's long success. First, it was always led by lawyers of solid integrity who were not afraid to nurture colleagues who were better and brighter than them; second, its leaders established a system to recruit and renew talent; and third, its lawyers were different enough in character to contribute richly in diverse ways to the firm's growth and yet, however different each of them was, they had lots of camaraderie and took great pride in being part of the firm. From R&D's success story, I made sure that we recruited good people. We had to get partners to succeed us who could do better than us. And we had to create a system for renewal. The most important thing is to know yourself. If somebody can run your firm better than you, then hand it over to him or her. So, we built a philosophical structure which recognises talent and appreciates change and the need for renewal."

In an interview for the Singapore Institute of Architects 50th Year Anniversary book, *RUMAH 50*, Seow Chuan attributed DP Architects' success to its two founding principles: integrity and talent management. By 'integrity', he meant not only professionally but rightful attribution and acknowledgement of the contribution of the individual talents and efforts of colleagues and associates. "He proudly recounted, by way of illustration, that he personally insisted that Michael Wilford be jointly acknowledged with DP Architects in the RIBA (Royal Institute of British Architects) award given in 2005 for the Esplanade project even though Michael Wilfred and partners had decided to retire from the project mid way. This philosophy underscored what Seow Chuan said is the most important success principle he insists on; that unless talent is properly and justly acknowledged no architectural practice can attract talent and grow."

The focus of the interview was on Seow Chuan's practice in talent management, and how the founders must ensure that the firm survives beyond them. DP Architects is run by Directors, these Directors manage all aspects of the firm's activities. They hire, nurture, assign and if young architects are found to have suitable talents and are conducive as colleagues, they are inducted into the firm's self-renewal process: "To ensure revitalisation, everyone has a run out date. In fact, there are three such dates: at age 55, at age 60 and at age 65. At age 55 an underperforming staff or a shareholder's retirement is confirmed and the person leaves. The Directors however have the prerogative to extend a person's run out date beyond 55 to 60 and even beyond 65 if they deem the services of the person indispensable. The structured retirement system is designed to create space for upward mobility of younger staff and shareholders, offering them opportunities to rise up the ranks and to take on greater responsibilities with commensurate enhancement of incomes."

Seow Chuan's concept of talent is not one of self but of collective talent, the notion that "the totality is greater than the sum of its parts". Here, Seow Chuan was quick to point out that the ability to work together harmoniously is very important. Ego must not be allowed to get in the way of collaboration. This was and is his key cornerstone: teamwork.

"When we became DP Architects, the element of teamwork became stronger. More close-knit and tighter," Seow Chuan is emphatic, his voice sways with conviction. "Among Gan Eng Oon, Chan Sui Him and myself, we had full, complete understanding. It was firm before self. Even if someone brought the project in, or client in, he would not say this was his client, and keep the client to himself. The client belonged to the firm. He would share with the rest how he got the confidence of the client, and together we would build that confidence so that the client understood and knew that we were the best to do the project for them." William Lim was also on the DP Architects board of directors until he left in 1981 to set up his own practice.

"From 1981, Gan Eng Oon, Chan Sui Him and I worked closely and enabled talent from within the firm to grow," Seow Chuan remembers the 1980s clearly. He remembers the decade when stronger teamwork was forged in the firm, especially in the face of a recession, and then from 1985 to 1995 more growth, or what he terms as DP Architects' Golden Age. "By the 1980s, Francis Lee had joined DP Architects, beside Ti Lian Seng, Chin Thoe Chong, Teoh Hai Pin, Wu Tzu Chiang,

Dadi Surya, Lesley Lim, Vikas Gore, David Liauw, Jeremy Tan and many others. Together, we forged a new beginning for DP Architects, one that was able to grow the talent pool, and was sustainable, with continuous renewal of DP Architects. It became our culture, a way of work that strengthened bonds of friendship and understanding amongst its leadership."

Ahead of design firms of the time, succession planning was also set in motion in the mid-1990s, with the firm actively formulating the concept of Chairmanship and CEO-ship. It was at this defining juncture that the third generation of leadership under Francis Lee was nurtured and groomed. Gan Eng Oon was named Honorary Chairman in 1999 and Chan Sui Him became CEO of DP Architects from 1999 to 2004. In March 2004 Gan Eng Oon retired, followed by Seow Chuan, who also retired in November 2004.

Chan Sui Him succeeded Gan Eng Oon as Chairman from 2004 to 2015 and Francis Lee succeeded as CEO from 2004 to 2015. It was a newly inspired DP with Francis Lee as CEO and Chan Sui Him as Chairman. Under their leadership, the firm grew from 300 staff to over a thousand.

Chan Sui Him retired in 2015, and Francis Lee succeeded him as Chairman from 2015 to 2020. Angelene Chan became the CEO from 2015 to 2020. Under their leadership, DP further grew from strength to strength. DP Architects has grown from a handful of young, ambitious architects to the global, multi-disciplinary practice it is today. While the firm has expanded beyond just architectural services and now spans across 17 offices worldwide with projects spreading across the entire globe, the core tenets of the firm have remained consistent throughout its history, which is often referred to as the 'DP spirit'. Since the very beginning, there has been a core belief in the collaboration of many talented people to create an environment of excellence and varied expertise. This allows the firm to weather difficult situations, as well as allowing design flexibility not typically seen in a principle-led studio. Over 50 years, DP has cultivated this collaborative studio culture, and it has been passed down through many DP generations.

Today, DP Architects is led by the fourth and fifth generation with Angelene Chan as the Chairman from 2021 and Seah Chee Huang as the CEO, also from 2021. With a new generation of leaders now firmly in place, DP Architects is stronger and better positioned than ever to push the limits. DP Architects is a happy firm with 'built-in' concerns for people. The story of how DP prevailed and overcame difficult times through teamwork and the display of DP spirit, has been told through personal accounts of DPians who have stayed with the firm through good and bad times.

With these values and sustainable policies, the firm has been able to evolve organically during the period of nation-building and develop a national pluralistic identity in architecture. While still a constant work-in-progress after 50 years, the firm's values and policies entrenched in all DPians will carry the firm to the next 50 years.[1]

The innovative and progressive spirit is abundantly displayed in the current management. See attachments at the end of this chapter — essays by Angelene Chan and Seah Chee Huang published in *a+u Architecture and Urbanism Asia Edition 2019.*

In 2017, DP Architects celebrated 50 years since it was founded in 1967. A rare achievement. Seow Chuan looks down at a publication on the table, *DP Architects, 50 Years Since 1967*. "Half a century, a real milestone." He takes in a deep breath and smiles. "At the DP50 Gala,

[1] DP Architects 50 Years Since 1967 by Artifice Books on Architecture, published in 2017. Artifice books on architecture 10a Acton Street, London, WC1X 9NG United Kingdom.

I gave an address as its co-founder. I said our aspiration since 1967 was to produce architecture of excellence that uplifts the human spirit. We dreamt big and led the innovation in design and planning with People's Park Complex and Golden Mile Complex. By the mid 70s, as DP Architects, we had steadily established a reputation for delivering well-designed, large scale mixed-use projects. By the early 80s, this reputation was sealed when DP Architects was appointed the architect for Marina Square, then the largest development of its kind in Singapore. It was also during the 80s the DP encountered perhaps its worst crisis — the economic recession. Everyone made sacrifices to keep the firm going. The demonstration of compassion and team spirit — what we now call the DP spirit — the practice. The 1990s was a period of consolidation. Then over the next decade, DP saw its biggest expansion, growing from 300 staff at the start of the millennium to over a thousand in 2010. Over the eventful half-century, DP weathered three big recessions, and each time we emerged stronger. I remember likening DP to a tree we loved and cared for. We watered it and gave it nutrients. The tree bore fruits and sowed new seeds. Nurturing each of them, we have grown new trees and at its 50-year stage, developed DP into a garden. To keep the garden healthy, we must continue to enrich and cultivate the firm. If we lose the love for DP and take out more than we put in, the trees will die. Love is at the heart of leadership, the importance of this cannot be underestimated."

The DP story inspires. Cradled from such humble beginnings, it is now a global brand. The development and expansion of the firm has been nothing short of meteoric. Yet in the minds of some, perhaps something is lost in the transition and expansion. During the transition from Design Partnership to DP Architects, did the firm lose something special? What about the individuality and brand of each architect?

Design Partnership had been a boutique brand. All that individualism and character of Design Partnership had now been swept into DP Architects, a big corporate entity, a firm of many architects — and perhaps no specialisation, no signature style.

Seow Chuan shakes his head slowly; he disagrees. "When DP Architects grew bigger and bigger, and now one of the biggest consultancies in the world, we did all kinds of work, but there is no single signature style. We had several signature styles depending on the context of the site and client's brief." His voice wears no apology. "Some architects say a big firm cannot do good work, that is simply untrue. It is also a fallacy to say smaller firms do better work. If signature works are defined as iconic works, I have one caution, don't let style get in the way of function. I always say good architecture is how well the architect plans and designs the space, not just how beautiful the form is. To us in DP Architects, we fulfil the client's requirement of space and function, and whenever possible provide the space in such a way that uplifts the human spirit. Architecture is never a single person job, a building is planned, designed and executed by a group of specialists, not one person. When Design Partnership became DP Architects, the individualism and the jostle for individual recognition was replaced by true teamwork. And it is the best way of going about the job because we also want the firm to survive after we are gone. This is what succession planning is all about. A corporate identity enables you to have many viewpoints, many concepts and many ideas, and we always need a plurality of ideas because no two situations are identical. We are always entering new situations and new scenarios, encountering new problems. That's why, through DP Architects, we could create this global practice with 17 global studios, with one global HQ. With technology you can collaborate across time zones."

On 7 March 2023, the Pritzker Architecture Prize, regarded as the 'Nobel of architecture', announced its winner for 2023. Throughout its 44-year history, the Pritzker has often been awarded to individuals with distinct design signatures: Frank Gehry's irregular forms, Zaha Hadid's sweeping curves and Tadao Ando's textural concrete. So, it may be a sign of the times when 2023's laureate, Sir David Chipperfield, was praised by the prize's judges for precisely the opposite.

"A gifted architect can sometimes almost disappear," read the jury's citation, as the 69-year-old was unveiled as the latest recipient of his profession's highest honour. "We do not see an instantly recognisable David Chipperfield building in different cities," it added, "but different David Chipperfield buildings designed specifically for each circumstance."

This was also reported on CNN. A quick check, and CNN had seen it fit to devote considerable space to this news, and made a resounding case for his "lack of a signature style":

> *Although best known for cultural institutions, like Des Moines Public Library in Iowa, the UK's Turner Contemporary Gallery and his reimagined Neues Museum in Berlin, the English architect's firm has completed over 100 buildings around the world. Spanning residential, commercial and public uses, the understated works are not defined by trademark motifs but by Chipperfield's insistence on answering what he calls the unique 'questions' posed by each project.*[2]
>
> *"I'm not that interested in architecture as an autobiographical exercise," he said on a video call from London. "We are sort of a midwife in this process. When we finish a building, we go home — we leave it, and it belongs to somebody else and we're not there to justify it and sell it anymore. It has to sell itself."*

---

[2] https://www.cnn.com 7 Mar 2023 "Pritzker Prize 2023: David Chipperfield wins 'Nobel of Architecture'.

Speaking to CNN ahead of Tuesday's announcement, Chipperfield partly — and modestly — attributed his approach to a "lack of talent", describing himself as "not an original genius in the way some, like Frank Gehry, are." He also recognised that architects often have little choice but to stamp their identity on their work. "Architects have become products. And products have to be distinguishable from each other," he said, adding: "So, they profile themselves, shape themselves and present themselves in slight opposition to each other. In a way, their signature and their autograph become part of their branding, and therefore their corporate and commercial success. I've somehow been shy of that, or at least I found that counterproductive."

As the prize's jury attests, Chipperfield's apparent lack of ego (in an industry that often glorifies great individuals) has proven an asset. He is the latest in a string of Pritzker laureates with few, or even no, conventionally iconic buildings to their names. Last year's prize was awarded to Burkina Faso-born Francis Kere, whose career has been largely committed to schools, health centres and community facilities in Africa. The year before, design duo Anne Lacaton and Jean-Philippe Vassal, best known for renovating France's post-war social housing buildings, claimed the honour.

First awarded to American architect Philip Johnson in 1979, the Pritzker Prize continues to recognise what it describes as architects' "consistent and significant contributions to humanity and the built environment." But within the broad remit, the merits on which winners are judged appear to be evolving. So, might Chipperfield's victory herald a wider shift, not only in architecture, but society at large?

"I hope you're a little bit right," Chipperfield said. "The period distinguished by the sort of 'icon' architecture of the last 30 years — I'm hoping that's a bit in the past now. It does, within the

perspective of sustainability and social inequality, start to look a little bit irrelevant."

Seow Chuan beams. David Chipperfield seems to be aligned to everything he believes architecture should be. He looks at the CNN report and reads out, "What unites these seemingly disparate forms is a respect for each site's context and an emphasis on process. How a building was made, why it was made, what it was made from and who it was made for should, Chipperfield said, matter more than the 'beauty parade estimation of architecture as image'... In our culture, the visual has dominated because it's much easier to see a building on the front of an in-flight magazine than it is to experience it... I think we are shifting now. And I think the visual and the formal will become very subordinate to process. How we build, what we build, where the materials come from — the whole supply chain, both in terms of sustainability and even in terms of ethics — will become the important things. And we will see beauty in a different way. Architecture is about experience and substance, more than fleeting imagery."[3]

He puts down the CNN report. I can see from his face that he is relieved. Finally, a shift is taking place.

Three Atrium Hotels and the Biggest Mall

While the transition to DP Architects saw changes in its architectural practices, Singapore itself was undergoing a period of rapid change in nearly every aspect. After achieving independence in 1965, the government wasted no time in enacting measures to address the basic needs of a young country, including its housing shortages and its low

[3] "Pritzker Prize 2023: David Chipperfield wins 'Nobel of architecture" by Oscar Holland, CNN, 7 March 2023.

educational levels. It knew it needed to spur the growth of manufacturing and bolster the advantages of its port to quickly make the country self-sufficient and alleviate massive unemployment. When these fundamentals were addressed and key infrastructure laid, foreign investment started to flow in, which necessitated a skilled, multi-racial, English-speaking workforce. A new breed of industries blossomed, focusing on the refining of raw materials, as Singapore had no natural resources to compete with its larger neighbours.

While the country had nearly a decade of unstoppable double-digit GDP growth after its independence, the 1973 oil crisis embargo and the ensuing escalation of oil prices had major effects on the progress of Singapore, which had by this time become the third largest oil refining centre in the world. The crisis crashed the stock market, and many construction projects were postponed or cancelled due to fears of instability. The fallout from the oil crisis sent Singapore's economy into a period of slow growth, plunging the country into two years of single-digit progress. Although the economy rebounded towards the end of the 1970s, the oil crisis showed clearly that the dependence on a single industry created a high-risk environment that could wipe out the strong foundation Singapore had been building. The key for the country was to diversify into a wider range of abilities and strengths, in order to tackle any further unforeseen obstacles that might challenge the country.[4]

"The ups and downs of Singapore were mirrored in DP Architects," Seow Chuan looks down, his mind wrapping around the early years of the newly- formed company. "To go into other areas and bigger jobs, we realised we needed to work with foreign architects, this was

[4] DP Architects 50 Years since 1967 page 72—73. Data from World Bank Data, 1965 to 1975.

Architectural model of Marina Square.

THE ORIENTAL

especially so when the projects involved foreign investors and partners. We may know the problems of large projects well but we did not have the exposure and experience of these foreign architecture firms. Ridgewood Condominium was the beginning of the cooperation with foreign architects. Marina Square soon followed."

For Marina Square, DP Architects collaborated with the renowned architecture practice, John Portman & Associates. Marina Square was significant in that it showed the firm's ability to handle projects of immense scale and complexity. It was one of the most important milestones because it was their biggest and most complex project yet. "It was monumental. In fact, it was three projects, three hotels, in one. And then there was 'the biggest shopping mall' connecting all three hotels. The hotels themselves were unique, they have big atriums, a trademark of John Portman. SP Tao's company, Singapore Land, won the URA public tender for the land. He approached me, wanting DP Architects to be the Singaporean architecture firm working with John Portman. Tao saw it as an extremely complex and challenging project. The firm handling it not only had to be competent, but also had to be able to work well with the foreign firm, and most importantly work closely with the local authorities. Because of my experience, my team's temperament and track record of liaising with building authorities, he saw DP Architects as the right firm for the job, the firm that would make things happen."

With regards to working with foreign architects, Seow Chuan has a realistic approach and philosophy, "I think in life, and particularly in Singapore, at that stage of technological development, there was much to learn from those who have done more," he flips a file, and pages showing the interiors of the three atrium hotels unfold. "You may have talent, but you may not have the experience, the exposure. You need to be humble enough to learn. Learning is lifelong, at any and every stage of one's life. Even today, at 84, I feel I need to learn from people younger, people of 25 or 28 years of age. They may have something to say that to me is sensible, new and refreshing. That's why we have to recruit talent. And when these young people come on, not only do they have more energy, they are more in tune with the new world. The world is constantly changing. You need to be in sync with the rhythm of the world. And if you want to make things happen, you need to be practical and go with the flow."

Marina Square Shopping Mall was completed in 1985 on reclaimed land, as the first major mixed-use complex in the area, along with Marina Mandarin, Mandarin Oriental and The Pan Pacific hotels. Singapore's largest retail mall anchors the complex, with 59,000 square metres of retail space when it opened in 1986.

Six years later, DP Architects worked with Michael Wilford & Partners on the Esplanade — Theatres on the Bay. What was the difference between working with Michael and Portman? "Both were nearly the same," Seow Chuan breaks into a smile. "Michael, in turn, was also learning from me as he found me to be level-headed and practical, he also relied on DP's team particularly when it came to dealing with local red tape. He asked his architects who were stationed here to listen to us. We brought in the foreign architects to work as a team. We valued each other's ideas, inputs and contributions to solve problems and make things happen. We were working with Michael 10 years after working with Portman in the late 70s. In the late 1970s, we had less experience, so we could learn from them a lot more. As time progressed, we acquired enough experience to be equals. Now our architects are functioning as foreign architects overseas. I always tell our architects not to be wary of foreign architects. They will always need us local architects, we know local rules and how to deal with the government authorities. There is also the crucial aspect of managing costs, and keeping the project running on time. Both require the experience and knowledge of a local who understands local politics and culture."

Most Singaporeans are now familiar with the three atrium hotels in Marina Square. In the 1980s, the hotel lobbies in the three atrium hotels in Marina Square introduced a new kind of experience to the local hotel scene. The Regent Hotel was an earlier, smaller version. "When Portman built the Hyatt Regency Atlanta in 1967, it created a sensation," Seow Chuan begins. "Atriums became a Hyatt Regency brand and Portman introduced the concept to a few other chains outside the US. You don't look at Portman's work and feel nothing. It is architecture as entertainment, if you like. Structural drama, rousing and inspirational, that's how his work gets you."

Before Portman's first 'neo-futuristic' wonder, the 22-storey Hyatt Regency Atlanta, most hotel lobbies were essentially efficient customer pass-throughs. In Portman's hands, hotel lobbies became temperature-controlled gathering places where guests and visitors lingered. They ate, read, and snapped photos of the spectacular, vertigo-inducing attractions above their heads. In the US and also some projects outside the US, Portman broke the model of the corporate developer hiring the corporate architect by being both of these things himself. As a developer, he bought himself the freedom to build what he wanted. It was architecture of futuristic fantasy based on some simple ideas: that people liked big, open interior space, movement, light, colour, and texture; that they liked simple geometric forms, which could be twisted and torqued in all kinds of ways; and that they could be induced to spend time in cities if the buildings they found there excited them. In the

1970s and 80s, some of the urban cities in the US were in decline, Portman saw his hotels and buildings as crucial places to bring life back to the cities and urban centres.[5]

Portman considered the lobby a hotel's 'internal lung', giving visitors a breather from the congested, grubby, possibly dangerous streets outside. When asked by the *New York Times* in 2017 why he designed such theatrical thoroughfares, Portman explained that he also hoped to give people a moment of respite and joy. "You want to hopefully spark their enthusiasm," he told the *Times*. "Like riding in a glass elevator: everyone talks on a glass elevator. You get on a closed elevator, everyone looks down at their shoes. A glass elevator lets people's spirits expand. Architecture should be a symphony. I had thought a lot about hotels — dim, dark lobbies with a desk and newsstand. I wanted to do something different. I wanted to create almost a resort, a change of pace, to bring in nature."[6]

Portman achieved these goals by stacking the hundreds of guestrooms along open walkways and then orientating the walkways towards the vast atrium, lit by a skylight above. Lobbies, restaurants and public facilities were located at the base, like a glamorous interpretation of a public square. The form of the atria, invariably replete with concrete parapets, chunky brass handrails, hanging plants and, most familiar of all, a core of glass elevators, became an instantly recognisable trademark of Portman's. The effect is both cinematic and science fiction-esque.[7]

These hotels, with their massive lobbies, also allowed for and boasted

---

[5] "John Portman, the architect behind the soaring lobby atrium, changed the idea of a hotel", by Anne Quito, *QUARTZ Lifestyle*, 3 January 2018.

[6] "John Portman, Architect Who Made Skylines Soar, Dies at 93" by Robert D. McFadden, *The New York Times*, 30 December 2017.

[7] "John Portman's Singapore" by Ross Logie, *Cubes Magazine*, Issue # 70, October/November 2014.

spectacular pieces of art. Some of the most impressive pieces were by Americans Richard Lippold and Larry Kirkland, and Frenchmen Daniel Graffin and Antoine Poncet. Their works played an intricate part in the unique Marina Square experience. Larry Kirkland's stunning hanging sculpture for instance, was one of the major focal points in the Marina Square Mall. Made of shimmering acrylic, Kirkland's sculpture was surrounded by a spiralling walkway that connected the upper and lower malls. Visitors could reach out and almost touch it as they viewed it from all sides. Each acrylic element in the seven-metre-tall sculpture was just three inches wide, which, when multiplied by hundreds, would drench the area with reflected sunlight by day and softer light by night. The awe-inspiring hanging sculptures by Lippold and Graffin graced the atriums of the Marina Mandarin and the Pan Pacific respectively. Together they stood at almost 150 metres high, weighed 4.1 tonnes, yet appeared so delicate and airy that they might at any moment take flight.[8]

Seow Chuan's gaze is sentimental. "The atrium hotels were an expensive way of using space and some were critical of them being anti-urban. Instead of integrating with the streets and the cities, they created their own cities within the cities. But every architectural phase has its context and historical relevance. Portman was popular when major cities were in decline, his works addressed that, and were wildly successful beyond that. To this day, I cannot deny his sense of theatrical sensibility; he crafted drama out of space. Atrium hotels continue to be popular for travellers, and they are very effective as venues for events."

---

[8] Stunning sculptures abound in Marina Square's own art gallery, "UPDATE", Marina Square. Number Five 1985 MC(P) 166/8/84.

Five years later, in 1991, DP Architects was appointed as project architect for Suntec City, a fully integrated complex with over 600,000 square metres of gross floor area, including an International Convention Centre. It was a URA land sale project where the winner of the land tender was a team of tycoons from Hong Kong. It was another project on a massive scale: four 45-storey towers, one 18-storey office tower, a 6-storey convention centre, a 4-storey retail podium, a fountain (listed as world's largest in 1998 *Guinness Book of Records*) and an underground car park housing 3,200 vehicles. Completed in 1995, it became DP Architects' biggest project on record in Singapore.

In 1999, Suntec City was elected, not only as the Winner of the Commercial/Retail Category, but overall Winner of the prestigious 1999 FIABCI Prix d'Excellence, the equivalent of the Oscar Award for the real estate industry. A project unsurpassed in size and prestige, Suntec City became one of Singapore's benchmark developments in 1999.

DP Architects 50th Anniversary Exhibition at URA Center 2017. With the Guest of Honour, then-Minister for National Development Lawrence Wong.

Essays by Angelene and Chee Huang

Blueprint for Integration

by **Angelene Chan**

DP is fortunate to have had immense staying power ever since our founding in 1967. We attribute this to our design philosophy of enriching the user's experience and spirit through architecture while being sensitive to the building's immediate environment and socio-political context. Our drive to pursue such ideals is understood through the firm's unique partnership that embraces diversity and identifies potential. As opposed to a singular viewpoint and approach to architecture, we have developed a conducive microclimate for the integration and collaboration between teams, subsidiaries and offices beyond geographical and technical boundaries. This flexible environment encourages a symphony of opinions and ideas in the orchestration of logical and ingenious spatial solutions for people.

It is crucial for architects to understand the potential behind such a multivalent approach that prevents the practice from being myopic or afflicted with a superfluous prejudice towards any particular mode of architectural expression and methodology. In fact, this creative environment kindles operational efficiency and purpose of specific domains that supplement each other. The fluidity and dynamism that arises from such relationships are underpinned by our deep conviction in wanting to create meaningful and delightful spaces that contribute to the general well-being of society. To date, DP has been known to be well-equipped in dealing with mega projects, having reached a critical mass with rich experience in a myriad of building types. As always, we seek to build upon our experience and knowledge while deepening our understanding of the built environment through specialisation and critical evaluation of known typologies.

In an ever-changing and volatile world, it is certainly illogical to depend on stereotypes that insulate the practice from the real concerns and social paradigm shifts of today. We always question the programmatic and spatial requirements of building types. Typology is often relegated as a taxonomic classification for visual gratification and used casually without much deliberation or conviction. However, we believe that with critical understanding of typology, architecture can better adapt to changing socio-economic conditions and contribute positively to the urban landscape in the long run. We are compelled to see through this Herculean task as a custodian of the built environment. In celebrating our first fifty years and looking forward to our next, DP is honing in on three strengths as we map our growth trajectory — designFirst, People+Partners and One Global Studio.

designFirst

Design is steadily evolving into a more sophisticated and stratified creative process that requires specialised expertise and knowledge. Furthermore, technology is acknowledged as the catalyst in liberating the production, analysis and development of design. The proliferation and democratisation of big data is influencing a new generation of designers. Hence, it is imperative for the profession to embrace this paradigm shift and its benefits to remain relevant. In DP, we organise weekly design critique sessions known as *designGate* for all of our projects, local and overseas, regardless of scale. During these sessions, appointed design directors consistently question the ideals of good and sensible design through rigorous and constructive discourse as we consider the changing needs of society at large. These formal critique sessions are coupled with weekly *designShare* — where thought leaders, industry specialists and DPians present and share their insights on rising socio-economic concerns, new material technology, and architectural thesis or projects as we widen our world view and develop our interests collectively. As a practice, we have a strong belief in the pursuit of good and sensible design given the direct impact our built environment has on our lives.

People+Partners

As a practice that relies heavily on human resources, it is crucial to constantly invest in our people by imparting new technical skills and knowledge that the industry is gearing towards. The continued development of our technical capabilities must be complemented with a critical mind through research and discourse. DP Academy was formalised as a structured platform to reinforce the firm's philosophy of 'Every DPian Matters' in the pursuit of self-renewal and excellence. All DPians are constantly learning to remain updated on the latest code requirements, material specifications and software capabilities pertinent to the practice. Technological advancement is accelerating at such unprecedented rates that it is practically impossible for any individual to master a wide assortment of skills. Technology also has the capacity to connect people across time zones and geographical boundaries. With initiatives such as *TodayMeet*, a daily introduction of fellow DPians worldwide, a large practice like ours can still remain closely knit as we know each other beyond work. The practice has always embraced the spirit of collaboration between our subsidiaries and fellow consultants as developing meaningful partnerships allows us to harness the power of *we*.

One Global Studio

Every building has to belong. Given how each project is subject to a unique set of conditions, ranging from climate to regulations, it is essential to sensitively localise the design to achieve its intended objectives. We appreciate the rich and multi-layered communication process in crafting a design to meet the needs of our users, clients, context and climate while contending with site constraints and challenges. Thus, DP's overseas expansion is predominantly based upon the geographical location of our projects as we tailor our services.

Today, DP exists as a group of companies with an ensemble of specialisations that cover a spectrum of delivery needs. Ultimately, we aim to leverage our extensive network of global offices to offer a localised design solution based on a holistic and integrated design methodology that encourages greater efficiency in delivery.

Moving in tandem with the nation's progress, DP remains responsive and adaptable. DP's specialisation through its group of companies further enhances the level of localisation in its services through constant and in-depth research. This encourages integration and collaboration as we deepen our understanding and heighten our sensitivity in the making of architecture. Liveable environments are products of happenstance and a creative vision from planners, developers and architects alongside the end user. A space has to be studied, inhabitants understood, and provisions catalogued. At this moment of introspection, we affirm our cherished design philosophy while constantly reassessing our design methodology as we continue to hone our capabilities for the future.

designFIRST

Celebrating 50 years of Design Excellence

by **Seah Chee Huang**

Design is thinking made visual. It is steadily evolving into a creative process that requires not only increased specialised expertise and knowledge, but also the use of technology in the process of achieving design excellence.

DP Architects was founded in 1967 with a deep concern for the built environment, with design and partnership as the cornerstone of our architectural practice. It is this people- and environment-centric design principle that has enabled DP to undertake projects in different contexts, local and international, in shaping buildings, towns, cities, and communities meaningfully these past five decades. Through these journeys, we have also developed our unique design-focused DNA: a suite of design expertise, approaches and initiatives that has allowed us to evolve the firm's design ecosystem — our designFIRST core.

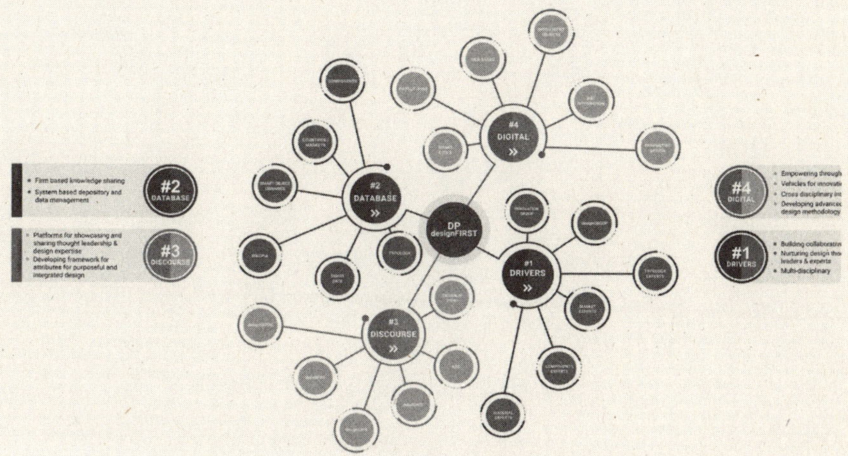

DP's designFIRST ecosystem is made up of four core areas, namely, drivers, database, digital and discourse.

DP's design ecosystem leverages on the power of 'we': the collective design experience and knowledge of DPians. This spirit of designFIRST crystallises into a foundational framework of four Ds — drivers, database, discourse and digitalisation.

Drivers

Central to the designFIRST framework are our very own DPians. Nurturing thought leaders and experts in multidisciplinary fields within the domain of architecture is essential for building a robust design ecosystem. A design group, comprising design leads and representatives, drives weekly design critiques and sharing sessions, championing design excellence within respective studios and team, to maintain standards and consistency. These design leads also serve as effective conduits for the sharing and transference of latest ideas, information, and knowledge from different projects or teams.

To further bolster the proficiency of our architectural practice, another thrust, designEXPERTISE, is also in place. Through these drivers of designEXPERTISE, the firm seeks to build on its design expertise and thought leadership in breadth and depth, developing key specialisations in 11 design typologies, namely residential, retail, healthcare, hospitality, education, office, transport and mobility, master planning, mixed-use developments, theme parks, as well as community and sports. These focus groups research and develop architectural designs unique to the typology clusters, leveraging on the wealth of DP's experience and knowledge through the expanse of such projects worldwide.

In parallel, the firm is actively developing various clusters of design expertise based on methods and materiality such as Design for

Manufacturing and Assembly (DFMA) and Virtual Design and Construction (VDC), as well as leads in geographical territories. In some cases, these core groups collaborate closely with external consultants and experts from research institutes and various institutes of higher learning to further enrich our design processes, systems and products, to strengthen our thought leadership in these design sectors. By tapping into our talent pool, the key is to further grow and enhance our design depository, to elevate our quality of design and nurture future design leaders to be eventual contributors and champions of our built environment.

Database

The sustenance of a robust and responsive design database — a knowledge-sharing and depository platform — is another essential aspect of designFirst.

Our design database is chiefly categorised into two groups: typology and component. The typology database is a shared knowledge depository comprising inputs from typology research groups within the firm. This depository is an extension of the typology drivers' initiative that pursues evidence-based design trends and solutions that are tailored to each building type. In each typology category, related information such as design norms, templates, 3D libraries, precedents and benchmarks, specific codes and compliance, trend studies as well as other unique requirements that will influence design and planning are collected and organised. This database also facilitates the sharing of information within the firm.

In addition to a typology-related knowledge base, the components database is a system-based depository which contains a collection of design standard details, components and intelligent object libraries and materials research. Our unique DP database, consisting of the firm's past decades of positive design solutions, ensures that the accumulated knowledge is well-organised, categorised for effective sharing and knowledge transfer to various teams in DP. The creation of a strong database makes certain that design processes can be streamlined, with compliant and workable solutions made readily available. In this way, consistency, proficiency and the quality of our design work can also be better enforced and maintained.

Discourse

Discourse is another key element in the design ecosystem as the industry evolves steadily, and the availability of current and credible information is critical to the function of an architecture firm.

Platforms to showcase thought leadership and trade design expertise have been introduced, promoting constructive and purposeful discussions among different teams. An example of such a platform is designGATE — a weekly design review and critique session led by the firm's directors for ongoing projects. This platform elevates the standard of design in the practice, by encouraging a culture of open discussion and cross-team collaboration. During designGATE, the projects are assessed with a key design assessment tool, known as the Attributes of Purposeful Design (APD).

The APD wheel is an assessment tool that establishes a set of purposeful design value systems to enhance the development of our core design ethos through four key design pillars: economics, environment, people-centricity and architecture. It functions as an effective and measurable assessment tool of design qualities, used at

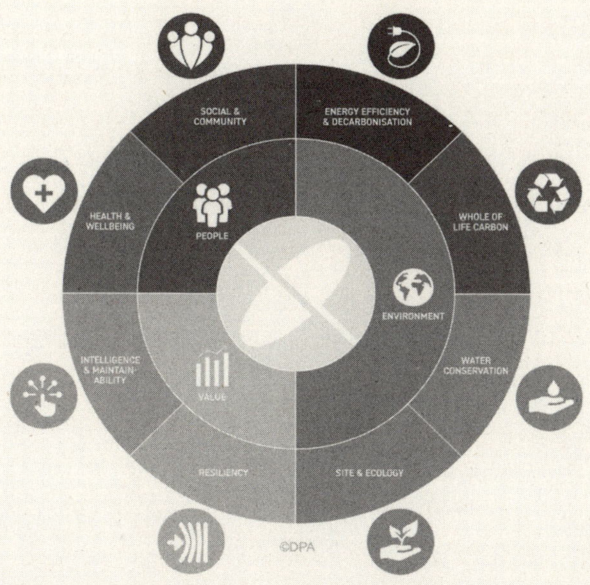

Attributes of Purposeful Design (APD) is an assessment tool to enhance the development of our core design ethos.

designGATE and review sessions, advocating greater consistency in design approaches among the teams. The APD also helps to raise awareness and encourage increased collaboration among disciplines, i.e. the integration of sustainable design, landscape and engineering in the design process. This strengthens the development of subject specialists such as buildability and integrative environmental design. As a design tool, the APD can be used as an analytical tool for evaluating trends and inclination of projects or typologies, as well as benchmarking and optional studies, allowing a more evidence-based design approach.

In addition, the weekly designSHARE — featuring lectures hosted by peers and experts, and project insights by team leaders — serve as an extensive and informal platform for intellectual exchange. These presentations are recorded and shared within the firm, making the information readily available.

To extend the discourse of excellence in design beyond our doors, DP has also introduced our own periodical aimed at engaging our clients, industry partners, and the community-at-large, titled *Design in Print*. The quarterly magazine, available online and in print, showcases new and upcoming projects and their design innovations, as well as interviews with key personnel, covering a vast range of design and industry-related topics.

The latest of our efforts to push our emphasis on design discourse and recognise design excellence is the launch of the DP Inspire Award. This annual internal award celebrates inspirational and transformative projects within the firm, spurring teams to go beyond the conventional design practice and create invigorating architecture that delights users, captures the spirit of the place, and promotes positive change and inclusivity in design.

Digitalisation

The final thrust that completes the designFIRST framework is digitalisation. In keeping with the speed of change fuelled by the proliferation of new technologies, it is essential for the design ecosystem to continually evolve by embracing innovation. Our design-INTELLIGENCE initiative has been crucial in ensuring that the firm succeeds strategically and operationally through enhanced connectivity across regions and communities. Through technology, we empower active participation in our One Global Studio in vital sharing sessions and discourse, regular design charrettes, and moving towards developing virtual design studios to facilitate seamless collaboration with our overseas partners. Central to this initiative is the adoption of Building Information Modelling (BIM), with a greater advance towards adoption of productive design methodology such as VDC. As we progress towards the digitisation of our database, we aspire to revolutionise the way we design, collaborate, and communicate.

Beyond enhancing operations, designINTELLIGENCE is also an initiative that aims to empower our designers by equipping them with essential skills to fully capitalise on technologies as vehicles for innovation, to facilitate greater cross-disciplinary integration and the development of cutting-edge design methodologies. For instance, SharePoints were set up to foster explorations in the fields of digital fabrication, data analytics, parametric design, and the utilisation of virtual reality and augmented reality for visualisations. These tools further contribute to the exploration and research into areas of new hybrid typologies, digital prototyping and advanced geometry, investigated through experimental projects such as the Archifest 2016 Pavilion, *Rhizome House* (Amsterdam Light Festival), *Cada Cuba Huele al Vino que Tiene (Every Cask Smells of the Wine It Contains)* (Logroño's Architecture and Design Festival) and Project Bus Stop.

Looking ahead

In the past five decades, the progressive implementation of programmes and initiatives that collectively form our unique design ecosystem has empowered DP Architects to grow from strength to strength. As we look towards the coming decades, with the opportunities and challenges ahead, we are confident that with our core spirit, structure and system of designFIRST in place, DP, together with our partners, will continue to shape the built environment meaningfully.

"I am proud to be a member of the DP family, and to be a custodian of the founder's legacy of original thinking and collaborative spirit that continues to shape DP Architects as we grow and change."

Angelene Chan

06

Talking About the Founder

From left to right, Chin Thoe Chong, Seah Chee Huang and Angelene Chan.

Chapter 6

Talking About the Founder

Woon Tai Ho's conversation with Chairman Angelene Chan, CEO Seah Chee Huang and Director Chin Thoe Chong of DP Architects

Angelene: I have been with DP for 33 years.

Chee Huang: This is my 20th year.

Thoe Chong: I am older. I have been with DP for 36 years.

Tai Ho: *I am here to talk to you all about the life and times of Koh Seow Chuan at DP Architects.*

Angelene: I met Mr Koh for the first time when I was working in Australia and preparing to return to Singapore. During this period, DP Architects was collaborating with Mitchell, Giurgola & Thorp on the SAFTI Military Institute project. It occurred to me that joining Mitchell, Giurgola & Thorp to represent their interests in Singapore would be a suitable career move. It was in fact, Mitchell, Giurgola & Thorp who proposed that I meet with Seow Chuan, who interviewed me in Canberra in 1989. Subsequently, Seow Chuan recruited me and I joined DP Architects in Singapore six months later, in July 1990. My initial assignment was the Suntec City project, and Mr Gan Eng Oon and Mr Francis Lee were the project leaders at the time.

Thoe Chong: My first encounter with Seow Chuan goes back to even before I joined DP Architects. He was a tutor at the National University of Singapore School of Architecture. He was lecturing us, not on architecture but, of all things, on law, construction law. When I graduated, DP Architects was one of the firms that was more design-based. They were focused on generating good design, and had some avant-garde approaches. At that point, they were also the industry leaders. All of that attracted me. I did not work with Seow Chuan until Suntec, but it was Esplanade when I truly worked with him as he was the director-in-charge.

Tai Ho: *You said DP Architects was design-based. What does that mean?*

Thoe Chong: It has always been. DP stands for Design Partnership in short. It has always been about pursuing excellence in design, through strong partnership and teamwork. That was and remains our core business. When I joined, the firm had only 50 staff. Now, we have one thousand. In fact, before Covid, we were 1,200 strong. In a global survey taken several years back, we were among the top 10 biggest architecture firms in the world.

Chee Huang: When I joined DP in 2003, there were around 200 staff members. Mr Koh was beginning to take on a more advisory role at DP Architects during that time. To a young architect like me, he was this tall figure, one of the three leaders of Design Partnership who created ground-breaking architecture that effectively planted the seeds for the growth of DP Architects. He had and still has an air of distinction and humility about him.

Tai Ho: ***How different was it when Seow Chuan was a leader of the firm with Gan Eng Oon and Chan Sui Him, compared to the present day?***

Thoe Chong: Angelene, you should answer this. You have led the period of growth that grew DP from 600 staff to 1,200.

Angelene: Despite our substantial growth, we have remained steadfast to our core values that Chee Huang mentioned. Our journey has seen us evolving together, and today, our leaders have a close-knit relationship. In many aspects, we consider ourselves a cohesive family, deeply committed to one another's well-being and to the prosperity of our organisation. Our dedication to succession planning, sustainable growth, and the preservation of Seow Chuan's legacy remains resolute. In this regard, we have remained true to our roots, even as we grew from a modest to a large office.

The primary transformation we have witnessed pertains to our organisational structure. This change became imperative due to the diverse and specialised branches that now constitute our entity. We have diligently structured and organised ourselves to ensure unwavering adherence to discipline and the upholding of our high standards. It is worth noting that our growth into a large corporation has brought about an increase in corporate governance.

Allow me to emphasise that we bear the responsibility of safeguarding an esteemed brand, one that was conceived by Seow Chuan himself, later with Gan, Chan and Francis. Our aim is to propel this brand forward, to nurture it with pride and a profound sense of responsibility.

Tai Ho: ***Seow Chuan tells me that he started as an architect at a time when the government had very little faith in local architects. For most of what he did, he had to partner with foreign architects on mega projects or projects that Singapore had no experience in at that time.***

Thoe Chong: Yes, indeed. Singapore has always been an open market and that includes for professional services. In the earlier years, we couldn't extricate ourselves from that kind of framework. So, we needed to compete or strategically join forces with foreign firms. For Marina Square it was a collaboration with John Portman, and for Temasek Polytechnic and later Esplanade, we collaborated with Michael Wilford — just to give some examples.

Angelene: Seow Chuan is right. During our early years, when we lacked experience in designing theatres or some new building typology, we actively sought partnerships with foreign experts to gain valuable knowledge. This acquisition of knowledge has been painstakingly built up over the years. Therefore, if one examines our recent portfolio, it becomes evident that our substantial accumulation of knowledge and hands-on experience has enabled us to now independently undertake a multitude of building projects. This expanded capacity has not been limited to Singapore alone; we have successfully executed projects in various international locations, underscoring our ability to handle diverse design challenges with confidence and competence. But, in the early years, it was a necessary move to gain experience.

Tai Ho: *At what point did that change?*

Chee Huang: The government's approach has definitely evolved over the years as our nation and industry has matured. Local architecture firms and talents have grown and elevated our skills and competencies; hence we have had much more opportunities in key bids and projects. The public sector agencies have also begun to recognise the importance of building a strong local talent base and capacities through some of these significant projects.

Angelene: Yes, while we partner with some internationally-renowned architects, we also engage in competition with them and occasionally emerge victorious, both within the confines of Singapore and beyond. In Singapore, one of the good points is that public sector design-tender bids continue to maintain a high degree of transparency and openness.

Tai Ho: *Do you think, when you have a massive project like Marina Bay Sands for instance, that the government should keep it to just local architects?*

Angelene: As Singapore remains an open-market competitive economy, in the context of design competition, I can see the reasons behind Singapore remaining accessible to the global design community, to bring the best designs and ideas to our city. Therefore, DP's primary goal is to continue to elevate our standards to the highest global benchmarks, thereby enabling us to remain competitive and excel within this environment.

Tai Ho: ***Let's bring our focus back to Seow Chuan. If I were to ask you to give me an adjective to describe him, what would it be?***

Angelene: Magnanimous.

Thoe Chong: For a high-profile person, he is unassuming, very in touch with the ground. Very accessible.

Chee Huang: I agree. Humility is the key quality of Mr Koh's that I am most impressed by. He has certainly earned bragging rights in the transformation of the architecture and art scenes, yet I've seldom heard Mr Koh talk about his own accomplishments except when asked. Most of what I know of his many achievements and philanthropy, I have heard from others or read in articles.

Tai Ho: ***What did he do for DP Architects that has now become a signature of DP Architects and a legacy of Koh Seow Chuan?***

Angelene: Are you familiar with DP's corporate constitution? I associate Seow Chuan with future building. He ensured that DP would grow from strength to strength in the future years. It is not uncommon for founders to centre a company's legacy around themselves, but Seow Chuan exhibited remarkable foresight and vision in ensuring the enduring success of DP Architects.

According to our corporate constitution, individuals are mandated to initiate the process of relinquishing their shares once they reach the age of 60. By the time they reach 65, their shares must be reduced to zero. This deliberate provision is designed to facilitate the transference of leadership to younger members of our team, granting them the opportunity to assume ownership of the firm.

By contrast, many firms witness their elderly owners and founders retaining their shares until they are quite advanced in age, sometimes even until their passing. Consequently, the younger associates working within such organisations often never experience the privilege of ownership.

Thoe Chong: Seow Chuan knows when to walk away. I am sure it was difficult to let go, but he did it for the long-term good of the firm.

Angelene: Hence I articulated the term "magnanimous". It necessitates a benevolent founder to willingly acknowledge that, at the age of 60, one's ownership stake diminishes, and by 65, it diminishes entirely. This commitment is enshrined in our corporate constitution, mandating that each of us adheres to this practice, thereby facilitating the transfer of our ownership stakes to younger colleagues, typically in their 40s. This deliberate action serves as a potent motivator for our younger associates, compelling them to invest their utmost efforts in the company's prosperity. I perceive this as a manifestation of astute long-term succession planning, fostering the enduring growth and sustainability of DP Architects.

However, this transition does not signify a complete disengagement from the organisation. One can still maintain a position as a senior director and receive compensation through alternative means.

I commend this practice as it embodies the epitome of honour and selflessness. It entails relinquishing ownership of the very company one founded, thereby affording the younger generation the opportunity to steer the organisation's growth. We can count ourselves exceedingly fortunate to have a founder of Mr Koh's calibre guiding our path.

Thoe Chong: That is the key component of the constitution, it shows he had the foresight to ensure the sustainability of the firm, into perpetuity.

Chee Huang: Mr Koh ensured that DP wasn't going to be just a one-generation firm, but a multi-generational one. I am a fifth-generation beneficiary and, with my partners, a custodian of the firm for future generations, so I appreciate what a tremendous task it was for Mr Koh. When I took over the CEO role from Angelene, I was mindful of the huge shoes to fill, left by previous leaders like Mr Koh, Mr Gan, Mr Chan, Francis and Angelene. On top of that, I began my stint as Deputy CEO in Jan 2020 and then as CEO in Feb 2021, when the Covid pandemic was still dominating headlines around the world. It was, and remains a huge challenge to steer the organisation through the weakened economy, and our industry is still in recovery from the crisis. I was able to relate my own experience to past accounts from Mr Koh about the crises and struggles that DP has weathered over the years. The Covid crisis deepened my appreciation and respect for the gumption and grit that Mr Koh and past DP leaders have demonstrated through the challenges of their time. Consistent to these experiences is the DP spirit of courage, teamwork and pursuit of excellence that Mr Koh often emphasised, that allowed us to prevail and emerge stronger each time. Indeed, we are defined less by the challenges, but more by the way we act and respond.

Angelene: The other day, during a conference, we were chatting with friends from other organisations. When Chee Huang left, an observer remarked, "Your CEO is very young!" In response, I conveyed our steadfast commitment to succession planning, emphasising our proactive approach to nurturing the younger generation within our ranks. It is our ardent belief that by investing in the development of emerging talent while our more seasoned leaders remain actively involved, we fortify the enduring competence of our company.

Tai Ho: ***I have spoken to other architects, famous ones. I see a fundamental difference. The output of an architecture firm is very public. Most architects would say, I did this building, I did that building. But Seow Chuan would say he was part of the team who did this, did that. He sees everything as teamwork, not individual work. He has not succumbed to the temptation to claim or associate his own name to any one project.***

Thoe Chong: I think the 'we' and 'us' mentality is very clear in his approach. For him, the personality part, the ego part is always secondary. Most famous architects are loud; Seow Chuan has always been steady and quiet, but he did great work. When we partnered with foreign architects for instance, he would always remind us to credit our partners. And this applied to everything we do, including the slides we use for presentations. It is important to him to give credit where it is due. People would refer to a building as a Norman Foster building for instance, or a Zaha Hadid building. For us, they just refer to it as a DP Architects building.

Angelene: To this day, each member of our team at DP Architects refrains from using the singular pronoun "I". Such a practice may appear somewhat unconventional to some, akin to the usage of the regal "we". When delivering presentations, the collective pronoun "we" invariably takes precedence. Even our interns adhere to this custom, for they perceive our endeavour as a collaborative endeavour.

Chee Huang: The awareness of the power of the team has been ingrained in all of us. For the past twenty years, that has been the way I see and approach my work. It is part of our value system. I would like to share my perspective as someone from a later generation: the power of storytelling is something we cannot underestimate. For instance, the story of Mr Koh mortgaging his stamps to the bank to get the firm out of a very difficult situation. These are powerful stories that stay vivid in our minds. He has countless stories, from People's Park Complex and Golden Mile Complex, to the Esplanade, stories that foster the DP identity and sense of belonging because they speak of our common and collective past. When I first met Mr Koh, he was about to retire and was not as active in DP. But the stories I heard made him relevant. These are stories I will share with the next generation.

Tai Ho: ***Seow Chuan thinks of himself as a doer, the person on site talking to the contractor, developer and negotiating with the building authorities.***

Angelene: Indeed, during the initial years, he assumed the role of the doer. However, it is essential to acknowledge that he did not lack ideas. Particularly in his later years, when he had retired, his reservoir of ideas was abundant. Remarkably, even after his official retirement, he continued to diligently come to work daily. On numerous occasions, a number of us would approach him, seeking his valuable counsel. Personally, I frequently turned to him for guidance, particularly in areas where I encountered formidable challenges. He possesses and continues to exhibit exceptional qualities as a counsellor. His adeptness in active listening and proficient counselling is truly commendable.

Thoe Chong: The green architecture approach was often expounded on by him. After his retirement, in the project he designed and developed for his old family home, he realised the idea of medium-rise living in the tropics. That was an example of translating ideas into physical outcomes; his attempt in envisioning environmental response in architecture.

Tai Ho: *Also, unlike other architects, he saw how important it was to cultivate the relationship with the building authorities as well. In the early days, if you didn't know them, you didn't get to do things. In the early years, the ability to be in tune with the building authorities was survival.*

Thoe Chong: More importantly, he has the right temperament to do that. His temperament is almost un-architect. Most of the early pioneer architects were loud and showy.

Angelene: In order to excel as an architect, one must also possess a comprehensive understanding of the business aspects of the profession. It is imperative to acknowledge that architectural prowess alone isn't sufficient; a keen business acumen is equally indispensable. Seow Chuan, in particular, demonstrates an admirable equilibrium between these two crucial facets. He adeptly navigates the realms of business pragmatism and architectural ingenuity, manifesting his capability to deliver excellence on both fronts.

Tai Ho: ***What kind of a leader was Seow Chuan?***

Thoe Chong: He was a quiet leader. The sort that need not be on the stage, shouting his orders.

Chee Huang: He was strategic. Mr Koh's humility and calm demeanour belied many bold and astute decisions that made DP Architects the firm it is today. One such decision was to collaborate with foreign architects on projects like Marina Square, Suntec City and Millenia Development, in order to build DP's capability and set the practice's trajectory of growth. This strategy allowed DP to not only survive during crises where other firms had failed, more importantly, it enabled DP to grow, scale up and expand our capabilities so that we were able to design and deliver large-scale complex projects on our own. DP would be a very different practice had Mr Koh not taken the firm on that path.

Angelene: When he articulated the imperative of collaborating with foreign architects, it was consistently approached as a partnership of equals. We did not assume a subservient role, nor did we solely glean knowledge from them. Our engagement was invariably characterised as a balanced 50/50 dynamic, if not one weighted even more towards our local contributions. While our journey certainly entailed a learning curve, it never placed us in a position of subservience.

In fact, for foreign architects working alongside us, there existed ample opportunity for mutual learning. Given our geographical advantage within the tropical context, we possessed a wealth of knowledge to offer, grounded in our profound understanding of our local environments. Establishing a company, securing projects, and formulating a sustainable organisational framework necessitated a pragmatic, business-oriented mindset.

Seow Chuan created an enduring legacy for future generations to inherit and build upon. This is where DP Architects is exceptionally fortunate to have his visionary leadership to ensure the firm's continued evolution and longevity.

Tai Ho: ***Now that DP Architects is into its fifth generation, how is DP Architects different compared to other architecture firms? How do you feel when someone says DP Architects is so dominant today?***

Angelene: I do not believe that the concept of dominance has ever been a concern for us. Our primary focus has consistently revolved around striving to produce exemplary work. When we reflect upon each successive generation within our ranks, a recurring theme emerges: an unwavering commitment to continuous improvement, whether within the confines of Singapore or on a global scale.

Furthermore, we presently find ourselves at a juncture where we are actively engaged in various philanthropic endeavours. These initiatives span a wide spectrum, from mentoring the younger generation within educational institutions to extending our support to charitable organisations. In recent years, we have made a concerted effort to give back to society. In this regard, we consider ourselves fortunate to possess the means and resources to effect positive change.

Thoe Chong: Our core values are RISE, "R" for responsibility, "I" for integrity, "S" for self-renewal, and "E" for excellence. I think dominance is about achieving excellence in what we do.

Angelene: It is not about "I am better than you".

Thoe Chong: We want to be better versions of ourselves.

Chee Huang: Like Angelene said, we never sought dominance. The pursuit of excellence and the spirit of continuous learning is in our DNA, passed down from leaders before us, starting with Mr Koh.

Tai Ho: ***Apart from succession and teamwork, what else has Seow Chuan left behind?***

Thoe Chong: Apart from the constitution, someone mentioned something interesting to me about DP Architects. If you look at the larger architecture practices, homegrown, Singapore-based, many of them have gone through major change, restructuring, or they have been sold. DP Architects has kept the core very much intact. There were offers to buy the firm. But the conviction in the firm is very strong, a belief that it is still best that we run it our way. This has a lot to do with the legacy left behind since Mr Koh's days. They could have easily made the decision earlier to sell. So that's something quite admirable.

Angelene: This pertains to the care and sense of belonging within our corporate family, along with the responsibility we bear towards every member of our office. Even though numerous other companies have opted to sell, which could potentially lead to a substantial windfall, our shareholders have unanimously chosen a different path. They have expressed their desire to retain ownership and continue to operate in accordance with the principles of DP Architects. We take immense pride in our identity as a Singaporean company, one that we are diligently nurturing for the benefit of future generations. Once again, I believe this decision stems from the generous spirit instilled by Seow Chuan, emphasising that our actions are driven by a collective commitment to ourselves and the generations to come, rather than pursuing individual gains.

Thoe Chong: He was all about spreading the value of sharing and continuous sharing.

Chee Huang: The value of sharing and teamwork, and Mr Koh's selflessness in the face of crises, helped set the spirit of partnership in DP. Putting the firm ahead of personal interests is the foundation that connects the partners to one another and to the firm, and it is the compass that guides and inspires current and future leaders, so that we can continue to renew our practice in more sustainable ways, and remain steady and strong during changing and challenging times.

Angelene: He uses the word "love". Familial affection. This inclination is likely attributable to his strong religious convictions, as he diligently translates his faith into actions rather than verbal discourse. Although he refrains from openly discussing religious matters in the workplace, he frequently engages in conversations about love.

Chee Huang: He often joked about enjoying his "liquid spirit to allow him to better connect with his holy spirit"! Mr Koh's love for DP and his love for Singapore, love for architecture, the arts and culture, means that he is a person who cares deeply. This is a leadership trait that I admire. When we care, we take care of the people around us, the quality of our work, the consequences of our actions, the impact of our designs and buildings on communities and the planet. This is an important quality to uphold and cherish, especially in our increasingly fragmented world.

Tai Ho: ***Through the years, what episodes with Seow Chuan do you remember most? Can each of you share some anecdotes?***

Thoe Chong: During my time working with Seow Chuan on the Esplanade, I witnessed his respect for people and concern for the community. We had some small group discussions where he shared how he saw Singapore, that Singapore should retain the spirit of the land that the performance art centre would occupy. He spoke passionately and told stories of the Satay Club, of life there before the site was cleared for the art centre. And that led to Esplanade — Theatres on the Bay being porous, being a space that people feel comfortable to go to, rather than an ivory tower that people look at from afar. The stories he shared regarding spaces for the people were painted vividly in my mind. When the Esplanade was finally completed, I recalled some of his stories, and realised he had achieved what he had set out to do — that it had become a people's space. I learned from him that you need to inspire those who work for you with imagination and passion. Sharing the same imagination helps us to realise the vision collectively. That was quite powerful.

Chee Huang: I recall one of our conversations where he shared his decades-old practice of sending himself a postcard and stamp from every city and country that he visited, jotting down his thoughts and connection with a place and time. To me, it is a unique way of documenting life's experiences. Great leaders have unique ways of living their lives, recording their lives, things that we can learn from. Mr Koh shared that being a collector also made him a connector, that stamps connect the past to the present, and how they connect our city to the rest of the world. What resonated further was how architecture possessed a similar, perhaps even greater capacity to connect people and even change the world.

Angelene: I can recount my personal experience of being interviewed by him. We met in Management's office. He was the head of DP Architects, yet we had such a relaxed and casual exchange. During our conversation, he presented himself as a true gentleman, leaving a profound and favourable impression of the firm. To this day, I vividly recall this interview as it stood out as a memorable experience.

Another remarkable instance pertains to a particular space within the National Gallery, known as the Koh Seow Chuan Gallery. When I first encountered the space at the National Gallery, I was filled with awe. What struck me was his humility; he did not announce or boast about the space to anyone in the office. To me, this was a significant accomplishment, yet he downplayed it with a simple remark, "It's nothing lah," with full modesty. Subsequently, whenever I visit the National Gallery, I make it a point to take a selfie next to his name and send it to him, always eliciting a jovial response.

Another remarkable episode involves our pursuit of a foreign partner for a project competition at Republic Polytechnic. I approached him for assistance, and together we meticulously examined potential architects from around the world. I was aware of his close friendship with Fumihiko Maki, dating back many decades. He graciously composed a letter of introduction for me to present to Mr Maki, which led to my journey to Japan to meet him in person. This incident underscores his ability to maintain and cultivate valuable connections and friendships over the years. Although these relationships may not have constant communication, he possesses the remarkable ability to recall world-renowned names when necessary. Maki and Seow Chuan continue to hold each other with mutual respect which characterises their relationship. The rest, as they say, is history: we emerged victorious in the competition and later went on to collaborate with Maki on the MediaCorp project.

May I ask, were your interview sessions with Seow Chuan conducted in his house?

Tai Ho: *Yes.*

Angelene: That's a pity. When he was working in DP, his office was a sight to behold. He would be among mountains of paper and books, on his table, on the floor, everywhere. There would only be a small work area left on his table. And there were also many scrolls of drawings behind him. However, amidst the seemingly chaotic piles of documents, he possessed an unparalleled filing system within his memory. He would be able to produce specific documents on demand. It's quite remarkable.

Chee Huang: Speaking of Mr Koh's memory, I was actively involved with the Singapore Institute of Architects. I had the privilege of interacting with pioneer architects like Lim Chong Keat, William Lim, Tay Kheng Soon and of course Mr Koh. All of them had elephant memories and it is astonishing how they can recall events so vividly.

They were so clear in the way they responded to questions from younger architects. They recalled details, personalities involved, the twists and turns of what happened. But at the end of the day, what I remember the most about Mr Koh, and what struck me the most, is his humility. Whenever he describes his experience with DP Architects, you will never hear him say I did this or I did that. I would also like to mention his personal assistant, Dorothy Yong. She was his PA for more than 40 years and retired only a couple of years ago. She was one of the most approachable and lovely people, and a friend of everyone in the firm. She was his one and only PA; this speaks of the mutual loyalty and respect that he cultivated in DP.

Angelene: Unless you really know him, when you work alongside him, he would not tell you oh, I collect stamps, I collect maps, I collect art. Yet the truth is, he is actually a big collector, not just in Singapore but on a global scale. So, you could be working in DP Architects, but you wouldn't know these sides of him because he didn't think it was necessary to talk about them. I think he is just very secure; these are his interests, that's it. No need to shout or talk about them. He doesn't see them as things to boast about. They are just things he enjoys doing.

Thoe Chong: Most of us learn from him more through his actions rather than his words. His temperament is admirable. He is steady and none of us have ever seen him get angry or blow up. He is never angry, never loses his cool.

Angelene: Yes, he is cool. I don't ever remember him even being flustered, let alone angry.

Know Thyself

Seow Chuan did not only read widely when he was in school and university, he also participated in many extracurricular activities and sports, including chess, billiards and importantly, swimming. Many in ACS today remember how he created the swimming and water polo craze there. A coach was even keen for him to train for the Olympics, a challenge he did not take up. Why? Know thyself, was his reply. In architecture, stamps and art, he went all the way because he knew he had it in him to excel at the highest level in each of these areas, but not in swimming. Koh Seow Chuan might have done many things since he was a child and attained considerable success in most, if not all of them. In swimming, he knew how far he could go, and, more importantly, what he truly wanted in his life, which was a career in architecture. A less focused person would have been distracted by the allure of the Olympics.

Tai Ho: *When did you first start swimming?*

Seow Chuan: When I was 10, the doctor found white patches at the bottom of my lungs and told my family that I might be at risk for tuberculosis, TB. I needed to do more outdoor exercise, he said. I was playing cards, billiards, collecting stamps, everything was indoors. I was sitting down and I was reading a lot. Nothing outdoors. My brother frequented the Chinese Swimming Club and encouraged me to go with him and learn to swim. That was how it all started.

Tai Ho: *Did you or others around you realise quickly that you were a good swimmer?*

Seow Chuan: Not really. It took me a month to learn how to float, paddle in the shallow pool. Between 11 and 12, I began to be more enthusiastic about swimming. I went frequently to the pool. When I was 13, I was noticed. I was skinny and quite small, but I liked to pace myself with real swimmers, those training for competitions. The coach took notice. "This kid swimming on the outside lane has potential," he said. He noticed I was keeping up with the older and bigger competitive swimmers.

Tai Ho: *You were skinny and small? Weren't you a national champion?*

Seow Chuan: I did not have the typical physical makeup of a swimmer. I was smaller and skinny. By 14, I shot up and my body became fitter as I was swimming a lot more. The coach would come and pick me up in the morning in his car. I was swimming twice a day. I became the Under 14 champion. At 15, I won the men's 100m backstroke, and at 16, I broke the Singapore record for the 100m backstroke at the Singapore National Championship. That was when the media took notice and started writing about me. They thought they would be hearing a lot more about me.

Tai Ho: *You studied architecture in Melbourne. You continued swimming and you were quite the celebrity there.*

Seow Chuan: The swimming coach at the Chinese Swimming Club asked if I would like to train to qualify for the Melbourne Olympics. My priority was to get into the University of Melbourne to study Architecture. So, I went to a high school in Melbourne, Northcote High, to sit for my matriculation examination, which on passing qualified me to be enrolled into the Melbourne University School of Architecture. I contributed to to the swim team while in Melbourne University. A relatively smaller Asian beating the bigger swimmers there was a headline story. I swam for the University, and broke records there too. I got the Melbourne Blue, a Melbourne University award for contribution to Melbourne University sports. I swam until I was 19. I reached my swim peak in Melbourne, even though it was 'casual' swimming as I did not have that much time to train. I knew I wanted to be an architect; my focus was on architecture.

Tai Ho: ***Most athletes would give up anything to be given a shot at the Olympics. Couldn't architecture wait for a few years?***

Seow Chuan: Aristotle once said, 'Knowing yourself is the beginning of all wisdom'. The relationship you have with yourself is one of the most important relationships you will create throughout your lifetime. A relationship based on honesty and truth. I know myself and I am honest with myself. When I looked at all the Olympic champions, they were all of a certain size, bulk and they followed a certain training regime in order to get there. Firstly, I did not have the body size, secondly, I couldn't afford that regime because I didn't think I had a future in swimming. My future was architecture. I got into swimming because of the white patches below my lungs. I did not expect to break records or be a national champion. I think knowing yourself is important, otherwise you waste time and resources pursuing paths that can only bring you so far. While I enjoyed it, I knew I wasn't going to be a professional at it. The success brought some glory, and I tried to push it for as far as I could go.

Tai Ho: ***So, no Olympic glory. But what did swimming teach you, and how did those years in the pool affect your life?***

Seow Chuan: Swimming is about just doing. Learning the right technique, the right way of kicking, the right way to move your arms, the right way of breathing. Then the coordination between breathing, kicking and arm strokes. Everything must be synchronised, in harmony. So that was the biggest thing I learned. When things are not in harmony or not aligned, you can't do your best. When you push your body, you know what the human body is capable of, how far it can go before the first signs of stress appear. We are humans, so we have limits. Swimming allowed me to push those limits — how much more, how much further. Can I push myself to 80%, perhaps 90% or 92%? What I did physically I can apply mentally too.

Tai Ho: ***You are a proponent of teamwork. Swimming seems individualistic. How do you reconcile the two?***

Seow Chuan: Although I was an individual swimmer, I was also a relay swimmer. I swam for my school in the 4 x 50m, 4 x 100m relay or the medley. In the relay, you need to inspire your fellow swimmers, not just yourself. You need to tell your relay swimmers how they can improve, whether it is in the strokes, the kicking or the breathing. In teamwork, you push each other and learn collectively. Teamwork to some extent spurs you to be better, to coordinate better and to learn from each other better.

1955 Anglo-Chinese School Swimming Team. Pictured: Team Captain Koh Seow Chuan (third from left), Chiam See Tong (fifth from left).

1955 Anglo-Chinese School Water-Polo Team. Team Captain Koh Seow Chuan stands second from left.

Tai Ho: ***What was your fastest time for the 100m backstroke?***

Seow Chuan: My best stroke was the backstroke; my best time was one minute and 10 seconds.

Tai Ho: ***Apart from winning, what else do you remember about swimming today?***

Seow Chuan: My wife keeps photographs and newspaper reports of those swimming years. Good for my children and grandchildren to know. In fact, our grandson and granddaughter are training as competitive swimmers. While going through the photographs, I was reminded that former opposition MP Chiam See Tong was on my team. Aside from this, my swimming coach Kee Soon Bee was also a stamp collector. Before he passed on, he told his son and his wife, "My stamp collection is for Koh Seow Chuan."

A Head Start in Life

Anglo-Chinese School (ACS) Chess Team 1955.

ACS Stamp Club Committee Members 1955.

Singapore 150th Anniversary Stamp Exhibition 1969.

1972 Meeting in Singapore on Formation of Federation of Inter-Asia Philately (FIAP).
From left: Dr Kandiah (Malaysia), Dr Khorschid (Iran), Dr Ichida (Japan), and Seow Chuan.

1974 Singapore Stamp Club welcomes FIAP delegates to Singapore.
Seow Chuan is fifth from the right.

1988 World Postage Stamp Exhibition Praga Czechoslovakia International Jury.
Seow Chuan is third from the right.

1993 Bangkok International Stamp Exhibition official opening. Seow Chuan, Coordinator of Federation of International Philately (FIP), welcomes Princess of Thailand.

1995 Singapore World Stamp Exhibition. First major exhibition held at Suntec Convention and Exhibition Center. For a minimum donation of S$2, visitors were invited to 'Unite the World' by affixing specially designed stamps onto the face of the Mural. Donations were given to the Handicap Welfare Association.
Guest of Honour, then-President of the Republic of Singapore Ong Teng Cheong.

1995 Singapore World Stamp Exhibition.
From left: then-President of the Republic of Singapore Ong Teng Cheong, Koh Seow Chuan, Minister Mah Bow Tan, and Member of Parliament Ng Kah Ting.

From right: Keepers of the British Queen Collection, Sir John Marriott and his wife.

1999 China World Philatelic Exhibition.

1999 China World Philatelic Exhibition. Presentation of Gift to Seow Chuan, FIP Coordinator.

Certificate of Honor

VICE PRESIDENT OF FIP
FIP CO-ORDINATOR CHINA'99
MR. KOH SEOW CHUAN

FOR HAVING CONTRIBUTED SIGNIFICANTLY TO THE GREAT SUCCESS OF CHINA 1999 WORLD PHILATELIC EXHIBITION.

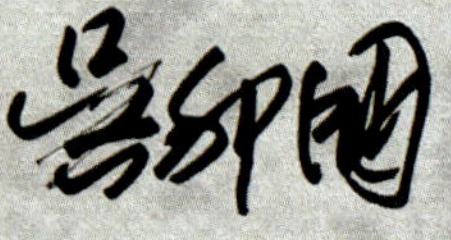

WU BANGGUO

CHAIRMAN OF CHINA'99 ORGANIZING COMMITTEE
VICE-PREMIER OF THE STATE COUNCIL OF P. R. CHINA

29TH AUG. 1999

Pacific 1997 International Stamp Exhibition in San Francisco, USA.
FIP Coordinator Seow Chuan, fourth from the left in the front row, with National Commissioners.

Singapore Stamp Club 60th Anniversary, 2000 and Launch of Philatelic Delights of Singapore and Malaya. Seow Chuan (third from left) is pictured with Hong Tuck Kun (eighth from left), Chua Eu Tiong (fifth from left) and Dennis Chua (fourth from left).

Philakorea 2002 World Stamp Exhibition.

Signing Ceremony of Patronage Contract between MIC PFK and FIP Seoul 2002.

2004 Singapore World Stamp Championship Opening Ceremony.
Guest of Honour, then-President of the Republic of Singapore S. R. Nathan.

2004 Singapore World Stamp Championship. From left: Minister Lee Boon Yang, Koh Seow Chuan, then-President S.R. Nathan and his wife Urmila Nandey, and FIP Consultant Joseph Wolff.

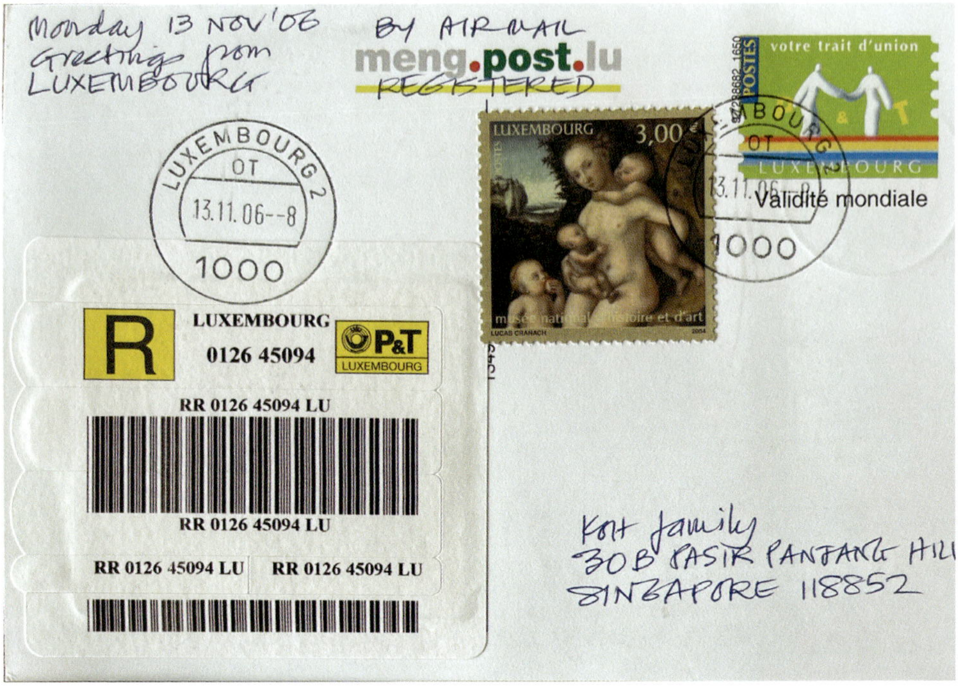

Monday 13 NOV '06
Greetings from
LUXEMBOURG

BY AIR MAIL
meng.post.lu
REGISTERED

LUXEMBOURG 2
OT
13.11.06--8
1000

LUXEMBOURG 3,00
musée national d'histoire et d'art
LUCAS CRANACH
2004

POSTES
votre trait d'union
LUXEMBOURG
Validité mondiale

R
LUXEMBOURG
0126 45094
P&T
LUXEMBOURG
RR 0126 45094 LU
RR 0126 45094 LU
RR 0126 45094 LU RR 0126 45094 LU

Koh family
30B PASIR PANJANG HILL
SINGAPORE 118852

In 2006, Luxembourg Post issued a special stamp and an official postal stationery card showing Seow Chuan (outgoing FIP President) and Joseph Wolff (incoming FIP President) shaking hands.

People's Park Complex

People's Park Official Launch and Public Exhibition at Victoria Memorial Hall 1968.

Esplanade – Theatres on the Bay

Foyer of Esplanade Concert Hall.
The design of triangulated glass and champagne coloured sunshades filters natural light for interior spaces and generates a dramatic transformation of shadow and texture throughout the day; at night, the forms glow back on the city as lanterns by the Bay.

The Esplanade Theatre, 2,000 seats.

The Esplanade Concert Hall, 1,800 seats.

Change and Consolidation by Design

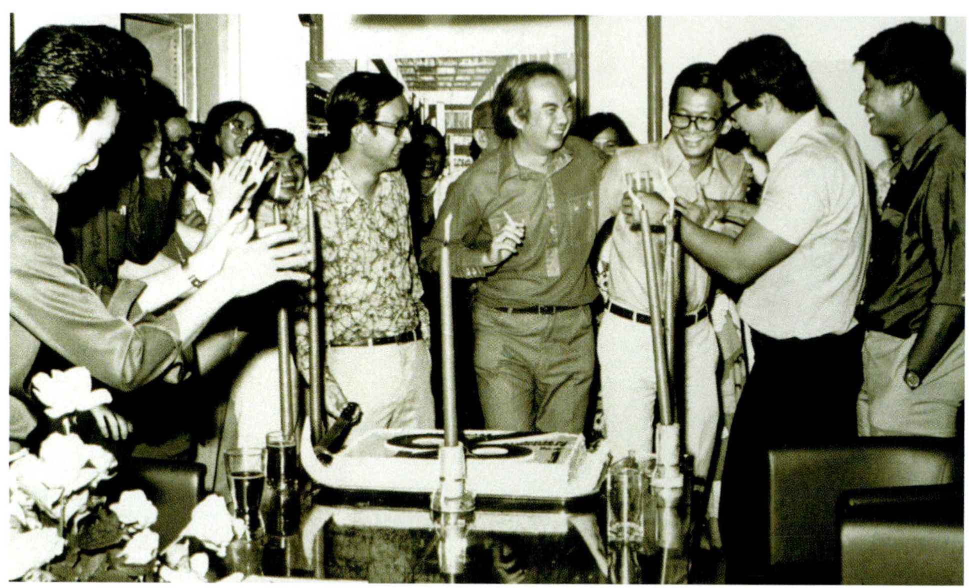

Koh Seow Chuan, William Lim, Gan Eng Oon and Tay Kheng Soon on the extreme right, flanked by staff during an office celebration in the 70s.

Chan Sui Him and Francis Lee in the early 80s.

Ti Lian Seng at DP Architects' Golden Mile office with his team members in the early 80s.

From left: Wu Tzu Chiang, Angelene Chan and Chin Thoe Chong in the early 90s.

DP Gallery was set up in 1999–2008 with the aim of promoting Singaporean artists and exhibiting good art from Singapore. From right: Chan Sui Him, Philip Ng, Gan Eng Oon, and Koh Seow Chuan.

Dr Lee Suan Yew with Koh Seow Chuan.

Kwee Liong Keng (first from right) and Chan Sui Him (third from right).

Senior Director Chan Sui Him (left) sharing a laugh with Founder Koh Seow Chuan.

From left: Chan Sui Him, Koh Seow Chuan and Gan Eng Oon hosting an Art Event at DP Gallery in 2000.

Chan Sui Him (second from right) having a chat with Teoh Hai Pin (first from right) and Ti Lian Seng (seated).

Angelene Chan (right) with Seow Chuan's secretary, Dorothy Yong (left).

2018 President's Design Award Singapore Ceremony at Istana. Angelene Chan received the President's Designer Award. From left: Koh Seow Chuan, Lena Lim, William Lim (seated), Koh-Lim Wen Gin, and Angelene Chan. .

Koh Seow Chuan with Angelene Chan and Francis Lee at the 2018 President's Design Award Singapore Ceremony at Istana.

Changi Airport postcard.

S.P.U.R. publications.

The *Thank You Lee Kuan Yew* portrait painting donated to the LKY 100th Anniversary Celebration by Koh Seow Chuan.

The *Goodbye Lee Kuan Yew* painting donated to the LKY 100th Anniversary Celebration by Koh Seow Chuan. The painting depicts the long queue of people from all walks of life, from celebrities and businessmen to hawkers and housewives, who stood in the rain to pay their last respects.

Collecting Art, Supporting Artists

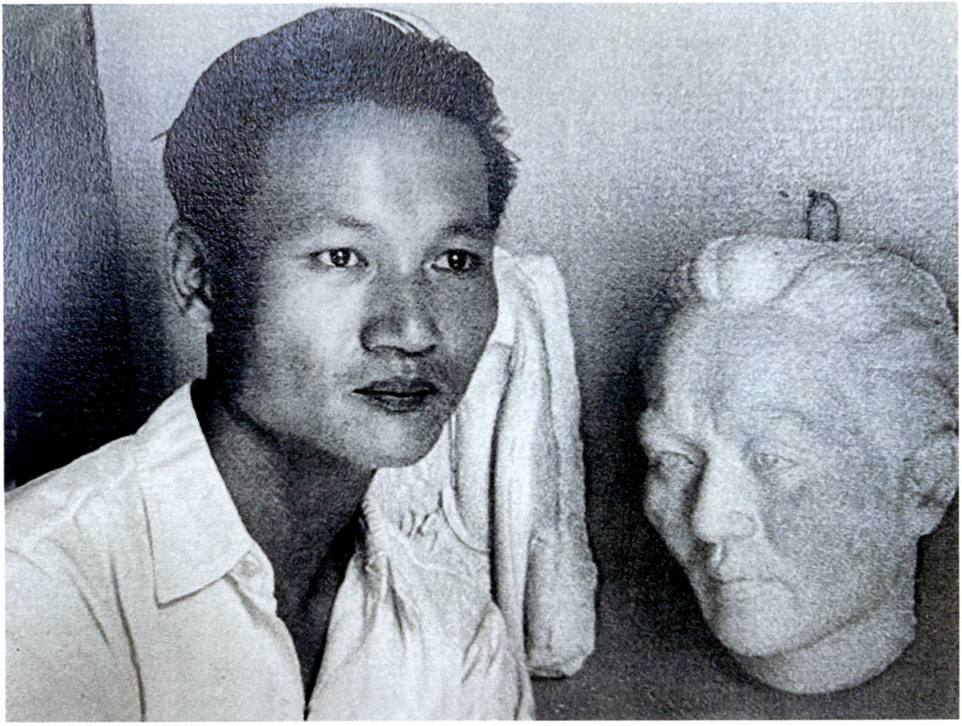

Artist Cheong Soo Pieng.

IMPART Collectors' Show 2018.

Balinese Village 1952–1964 by Cheong Soo Pieng.

A Patron's Role

Lim Tze Peng Exhibition at Singapore Art Museum 1998.
A loan from Koh Seow Chuan's Collection. Guest of Honour Tommy Koh.

From right: Lim Chee Onn, Tommy Koh, Mr and Mrs Lim Tze Peng,
Earl Lu, Kwok Kian Chow.

Lim Tze Peng Exhibition at Singapore Art Museum 2003. Lim Tze Peng and Koh Seow Chuan pictured here with Guest of Honour Minister Lee Boon Yang.

From right: Minister Lee Boon Yang, Tommy Koh, Lim Tze Peng, Mrs Koh-Lim Wen Gin, Kwok Kian Chow and Koh Seow Chuan.

Ink Expressions Exhibition 2011. Featuring 9 Singapore artists at Artspace@Helutrans, with the Guest of Honour, Jane Ittogi. From right: Edmund Tie, Kwok Kian Woon, Koh Seow Chuan, Jane Ittogi, Lim Tze Peng, Teo Han Wue.

Exhibition Opening of 'Soo Pieng in Nanyang' at Nanyang Academy of Fine Arts 2013, with the Guest of Honour, then-Minister for Culture, Community and Youth, Lawrence Wong. From right: Choo Thiam Siew, Minister Lawrence Wong, Soo Pieng's daughter Cheong Leng Guat, Koh Seow Chuan, Koh-Lim Wen Gin and Bridget Tracy Tan.

Exhibition Opening of 'Joie de Vivre' Chen Cheng Mei at Nanyang Academy of Fine Arts 2014. From left: Kwok Kian Chow, Lim Tze Peng, Chen Cheng Mei, Bridget Tracy Tan and Koh Seow Chuan.

Exhibition Opening of 'allegories' Wong Shih Yaw at Nanyang Academy of Fine Arts 2015. Artist Wong Shih Yaw with then-Minister for Culture, Community and Youth, Lawrence Wong (centre).

Vibrant Youth by Wong Shih Yaw.

Paintings by Artist Tang Da Wu from Koh Seow Chuan's Collection, exhibited at IMPART Collectors' Show 2018.

Koh Seow Chuan receiving the President's Design Award for The Esplanade — Theatres on the Bay in 2006 from S.R. Nathan, then-President of the Republic of Singapore.

Koh Seow Chuan receiving the Friends of MCCY Awards from then-Minister for Culture, Community and Youth, Lawrence Wong.

Mrs and Mrs Koh receiving the Distinguished Patronage of the Heritage Award 2009 from Minister Lui Tuck Yew. Seow Chuan donated 2,712 items comprising early legal documents, rare and contemporary monographs, hand-carried letters and maps of Singapore, Southeast Asia and Asia to the National Library Board (NLB).

Istana Art Advisory Panel 2011–2017 with Dr Tony Tan, then-President of the Republic of Singapore.

Lunch hosted by Jane Ittogi, Chairman of Singapore Art Museum 2009.

Official launch of National Art Gallery Open House 8 October 2010.

LaSalle Graduation Ceremony 2014. Minister Heng Swee Keat with LaSalle Board of Directors and Senior Management.

In 2017, Seow Chuan donated more than 9,000 social historical documents to the NLB.

Named as the Koh Seow Chuan Collection, Seow Chuan's donation became an important resource for researchers interested in studying the social and business history in Singapore.

DP Architects Celebrates 50th Anniversary at Suntec City Convention Centre.

DP 56th Anniversary Celebration 2023 (above and on the right) at Golden Mile Complex.

Koh Seow Chuan and Hsieh Fu Hua receiving the Pinnacle Award from Chairman Peter Ho, at the National Gallery Singapore.

ร้าน
ขาย
ยา
WE
ARE
HERE

"Lee Kuan Yew was the architect of Singapore's prosperity. There will not be another Prime Minister like him."

07

Lee Kuan Yew at 100

Chapter 7

Lee Kuan Yew at 100

A Prime Minister Who Listened

If Lee Kuan Yew were alive today, he would have been 100 years old on 16 September 2023. A Singaporean barrister and statesman, he served as the first Prime Minister of Singapore between 1959 and 1990, and the secretary-general of the People's Action Party between 1954 and 1992. He was the Member of Parliament for Tanjong Pagar from 1966 until his death in 2015.

"I had three encounters with Lee Kuan Yew." Seow Chuan's voice is crystal clear this morning. "There is no one I know who dedicates his life so completely to a country as Lee Kuan Yew did for Singapore. Everything he did was for the good of Singapore and Singaporeans."

When he passed away in 2015, *The Business Times*, under the editorship of Alvin Tay, invited captains of industry, heads of government agencies, CEOs and Managing Directors of MNCs and private companies to write in about their personal experiences with Lee Kuan Yew and how Singapore could best honour the spirit of the country's founding father. The paper received many, many letters. Alvin Tay could only publish 40 of them, and one of the letters published was Koh Seow Chuan's.

of hi

Koh Seow Chuan
Founder
DP Architects Pte Ltd

I am a collector of stamps and art, a postal historian, and an architect.

For this reason, Mr Lee Kuan Yew's defence of postal workers as a lawyer in the 1950s touched me deeply. It showed his concern for the common man, in this case, the postal workers. What was to make an even greater impact on me was how, even when he had become Prime Minister, he was still prepared to reach out and listen.

In 1971, I was invited, along with members of the Singapore Planning and Urban Research Group, SPUR, to have dinner with him at the Istana. He made time to listen to us — a group of architects, urban planners, lawyers and sociologists — and to discuss ideas for the development of Singapore.

The same preparedness to listen carried through over the decades. In 1995, I had the opportunity to present the design of Esplanade — Theatres by the Bay to him and the other members of the Cabinet. Although he was initially uncertain that Singapore was ready for a major arts centre and to allocate a large budget for its development, he was prepared to listen. He was eventually persuaded by his colleagues.

These experiences made a deep impression on me: A great man who, despite his intellect and farsightedness, still made time to listen and to learn.

For the 100th year anniversary of Lee Kuan Yew's birth, Channel News Asia (CNA) produced two documentaries on him, one of which is titled "I Remember". The approach of this documentary was to get people who had known him over the decades to recount their experiences with him. While researching for the documentary, CNA stumbled upon the letter Seow Chuan had written to *The Business Times*.

"The researcher contacted me when she found and read the letter." Seow Chuan looks at his wife, who has been helping him manage his time with the CNA team. "The team was interested to know about SPUR, our vision and mission, what we proposed and suggested to the government and Lee Kuan Yew then, and what his reaction had been. They also wanted me to recount the dinner at the Istana in 1971, who attended from SPUR, the ministers present and what Lee Kuan Yew said at the dinner."

Today, not many people know about SPUR. "I hope to use this documentary by CNA to inform people about SPUR," Seow Chuan begins in a low voice. "It was an important part of Singapore's history. SPUR stands for the Singapore Planning and Urban Research Group. You can consider SPUR to be…" he pauses to find the right word. "Perhaps it was Singapore's first think tank; we were a major voice on urban planning issues in Singapore in the 1960s and 1970s. We kept the membership small, between 10 to 15 members."

SPUR was made up of young professionals who were in their mid-20s and 30s. Formed in 1965, the year the country achieved independence, the members were idealistic and eager, all ready to contribute to the urban development of the country. SPUR had regular dialogues with government departments and the media. Views, proposals, suggestions and recommendations were made in the form of memorandums to government departments.

Foreword by the Prime Minister

PRIME MINISTER,
SINGAPORE

It is not without good reason that Singapore's reputation as a builder has spread throughout the region. It is in large measure due to the dedication our administrators, architects and engineers have brought to their job.

The S.P.U.R. Group represents a critical, but nevertheless dedicated, interest in the kind of Singapore we are building and bequeathing to future generations.

Once the back of the housing problem was broken by 1963, our targets were inevitably raised. The aim no longer was to house our people, but housing them in circumstances that make for agreeable community-living; besides the necessities, some privacy, attractive surroundings, and unity and intimacy of the neighbourhood.

I hope the Exhibition by the S.P.U.R. Group will stimulate public interest and discussion on these finer objectives we must achieve in our urban renewal and satellite town programmes.

[signature]

總理獻詞

新加坡建築事業的成就，在本區享有盛譽，決非偶然的。這主要是由於我們的主管行政人員，繪測師與工程師對於他們的工作，具有獻身服務精神的結果。

新加坡設計與城市研究学社的一群專業人士對我們現在所從事與建與留傳給後代的，是怎樣的新加坡，他們忠於所業，他們代表着他們的利害關係。

當我們於一九六三年成功地解決了房屋問題之後，我們隨即將我們的目標提高。我們現在的目標不只是為了人民提供住屋，而是提供具有適合集體生活環境的住屋；除了必要設施外，還須給居民有清靜美麗的環境和促進團結和親切友誼的條件。

我希望貴社是次所舉行的展覽會能夠激發公衆人士，使他們對於市區重建計劃與衛星市鎮興建計劃中的較高目標，發生興趣，並加以討論。

李光耀

Brochure of a public exhibition organised by Singapore Urban Planning Urban Research Group first held at Elizabeth Walk July 27 to August 4, 1968.

Seow Chuan's first interaction with Lee Kuan Yew was through SPUR in 1968. "Because of our regular interactions with government departments and the media on urban development issues, over time, there was sufficient information on SPUR's work and involvement in the public realm. We were sure Lee Kuan Yew must have followed the initiatives and the work of SPUR through the information available. In November 1968, we wrote to his personal assistant, asking him to be a patron for an exhibition we were going to hold, *Singapore Our Environment, the Past, Today and Tomorrow*. He not only responded positively, he also gave us a patron message which we published."

It is not without good reason that Singapore's reputation as a builder has spread throughout the region. It is in large measure due to the dedication our administrators, architects and engineers have brought to their job.

The S.P.U.R. Group represents a critical, but nevertheless dedicated, interest in the kind of Singapore we are building and bequeathing to future generations.

Once the back of the housing problem was broken by 1963, our targets were inevitably raised. The aim no longer was to house our people, but housing them in circumstances that make for agreeable community living: besides the necessities, some privacy, attractive surroundings, and unity and intimacy of the neighbourhood.

I hope the exhibition by the S.P.U.R. Group will stimulate public interest and discussion on these finer objectives we must achieve in our urban renewal and satellite town programmes.

SPUR was busiest from 1969 to 1971. These were the early years of the People's Action Party (PAP) government; there were many policies on urban renewal and planning and SPUR followed and examined them closely. "We engaged the government by giving them feedback, writing to them and attending meetings and seminars organised by them. Most of our ideas, views and activities were compiled into two books."

He picks up two publications on the table with *65—67 SPUR* and *68—71 SPUR* on the covers. As he flips through the pages, I can tell he is mentally going through the years the group was active with the government.

Among SPUR's most notable achievements was urging the authorities to relocate the airport to Changi instead of expanding it in Paya Lebar.

"By the late 1960s, it was clear that Paya Lebar Airport would not be able to cope with the growing traffic for much longer," says Seow Chuan as he flips the book to the page on Paya Lebar Airport. "Singapore needed a bigger airport, with at least two runways. The proposal put to Lee Kuan Yew by the government officers was to expand Paya Lebar and construct a second runway. External consultants too, recommended expanding Paya Lebar's terminals and building a second runway by filling up the nearby Serangoon River." He pauses. "We felt that Paya Lebar had inherent disadvantages. It was located near the city centre. Expansion would be limited. Worse, noise and air pollution would become worse because the flight path footprint was already over our city centre. I remember conducting noise pollution studies from different distances to the airbase to demonstrate to the authorities the impact of an airport near residential zones. We felt that expanding the airport would sterilise a large portion of the Paya Lebar area. What we proposed was to build a new airport in Changi, taking over the former Royal Air Force base there. Such an airport would be located away from the city centre and flights into and out of Changi would be over the water. In addition, there was the possibility of future expansion by reclaiming land. The airport issue was hotly debated, and some sided with the consultants. They felt moving to Changi would be too expensive, especially after including the loss of investment already made on Paya Lebar. I also remember that at the dinner at the Istana where core members of the SPUR Group were invited, Lee Kuan Yew expressed his own doubts about the expansion of Paya Lebar Airport. To be very sure, he appointed Howe Yoon Chong, then-chairman of the Port of Singapore Authority, to head a team to study if we could move to Changi in time before a second runway was necessary. And the team concluded that Changi was possible and could be ready by 1981. SPUR made its views known on many urban development issues, but our initial case for the Changi option was probably the most satisfying."

With SPUR's many submissions, the government departments were of course not happy. Not only did it mean extra work for the civil servants, the government also did not like to be told that their plans were not always well thought through. By the early 1970s, SPUR was less welcome, especially when it became embroiled in public debate and controversies over government plans and policies. It therefore came as a surprise when the key SPUR members were invited to the Istana for dinner in 1971.

"We were pleasantly surprised," says Seow Chuan. "Remember, I was only 32, and all our members were in our mid-20s and 30s. None of us had been to the Istana. I remember that eight of us attended." He pauses. Wen Gin has made him his usual, whisky with water. As usual, he shows his appreciation to her with a wide smile. "We began at the Istana with water and soft drinks." He looks at me and laughs. "Not beer or alcohol. We mingled and then sat down and there were two tables. I was at his table. He started by addressing to his team. He said, I have invited the core members of the SPUR group here to dinner. We can talk through how we can deal with what they have suggested. To his group of ministers and civil servants, he said that SPUR was a group of young professionals who had ideas; that not all of these ideas might be sound or relevant for Singapore, but they should be heard nevertheless. And that we should all talk and think through them. Listening to him, it was clear to me he did not want the government to come across as people who were closed and not prepared to listen. He said Singapore was too small that every talented person was important to the nation's progress. I remember, Howe Yoon Chong, Eddie Baker and Rajaratnam were there. The civil servants who attended the dinner came from departments overseeing the environment, housing, culture and transport."

Lee Kuan Yew would have been 100 years old in September 2023. On 23 March 2015, he passed away at the age of 91, having been hospitalised at the Singapore General Hospital with severe pneumonia since 5 February that year. In an emotional televised address, his son Prime Minister Lee Hsien Loong, paid tribute to him. "He fought for our independence, built a nation where there was none, and made us proud to be Singaporeans. We won't see another man like him. To many Singaporeans, and indeed others too, Lee Kuan Yew was Singapore."[1]

The US President, Barack Obama, called him a "true giant of history" while UN secretary general Ban Ki-moon called him a "legendary figure in Asia" and China's President Xi Jinping praised him as an "old friend of the Chinese people."

"He was the architect of Singapore's prosperity," Seow Chuan says simply. "He oversaw Singapore's independence from Britain and its separation from Malaysia. He co-founded the People's Action Party,

---

1 Prime Minister's Office, Statement by Prime Minister Lee Hsien Loong 23 March 2015.

which has governed Singapore since 1959, and was Singapore's first Prime Minister. I don't think there will be another Prime Minister like him." He pauses again, looks down and then back up at me. "Following the dinner at the Istana, I kept thinking of what the common perception of him was, his iron grip on power, how he restricted freedom of speech, how he dealt with his political opponents. Yet there he was at the Istana — very human, fair, very focused on the well-being of Singapore and Singaporeans. He was willing to listen to alternative views, so long as they contributed to help Singapore and Singaporeans. To his team, he said, listen to these alternative views, and if you disagree, I'll be the arbitrator. His entire life seemed to be focused on solving problems for Singapore and making sure people didn't try to incite conflict between the people of Singapore. He seemed very focused on issues and solving them behind closed doors, not in the glare of the public. At the dinner, he basically said, if you think there are problems, you can tell us. My takeaway from the dinner was that he was very committed to Singapore. He had a commanding presence, the real commander-in-chief. After the meeting, I knew he was going to be leading Singapore for a long time. He thrived on the politics of survival. During that dinner, I saw someone who would survive any opponent."

Seow Chuan was a moderate member of SPUR, one of the few who did not write any memorandum to the government departments or media. He did not contribute any articles to either of the two publications by SPUR either. "I was the unofficial editor," he says with a slight smile. "I made sure the articles represented most of the members of SPUR, not just the individuals who wrote them. What happened after the Istana dinner? Some members saw it as some kind of endorsement from the Prime Minister, and became very confident and started to push the government very hard. And that became our Achilles' heel. SPUR became embroiled in more and more controversy, and the key members became less united. SPUR was dissolved in 1975, because it had become too vocal."

Seow Chuan sits back, folding his arms across his chest. "So much has been said and written about Lee Kuan Yew," he smiles. "But honestly, through my three interactions with him, it was quite easy to work with him. Lee Kuan Yew believed in facts, data and logic, not theory or personal agenda. If you approached him that way, you would be able to navigate the situation effectively. For Paya Lebar vs Changi Airport, he went with the facts. In the Esplanade episode, he was eventually persuaded by the facts and supported the art centre. Then, with the National Gallery, he listened and accepted the hard truths, that the former Supreme Court and City Hall were sinking, and went with the budget we proposed instead of a much lower budget. [See Chapter 11] Lee Kuan Yew might have been many things, but what I appreciated most about him was, he accepted the fact that no one has a monopoly on wisdom. He believed in citizen participation, but of a certain kind. It must not be personal and it must be objective. And it must be based on data and logically put together. So, if you did your homework, you'd survive him."

Thank You, Lee Kuan Yew; Goodbye, Lee Kuan Yew

Some 10,000 trees were planted across Singapore to mark the 100th year since the birth of Lee Kuan Yew. He had launched the first nationwide tree planting campaign in 1963 and introduced the 'Garden City' vision in May 1967, which started a greening movement that lasted for decades.

On 15 May 2023, the Monetary Authority of Singapore (MAS)

launched a S$10 coin to commemorate the 100th anniversary of Lee Kuan Yew's birth. The coin pays tribute to Mr Lee's "strategic vision, boldness and indomitable spirit that transformed Singapore from a regional trading port to a global manufacturing, business and financial hub", MAS said in a statement. One side of the coin features a portrait of Mr Lee, accompanied in the foreground by the Marina Barrage. It represents his vision to build a freshwater reservoir in the city, strengthening Singapore's water resilience.

"In April 2023, I decided to donate two paintings from my art collection depicting Lee Kuan Yew as my contribution to Lee Kuan Yew's 100th Anniversary celebration. Lee Kuan Yew, as Singapore's Founding Father, was responsible for Singapore's success story and prosperity today. I hope these two paintings will be permanently exhibited in one of Singapore's national museums."

A great idea. I am keen to know more about the two Lee Kuan Yew paintings.

"Ah, the two paintings." His voice acquires a quiet clarity. "The first one I commissioned because I felt that Lee Kuan Yew was unusually committed to the welfare of ordinary Singaporeans. And for the success of Singapore, he needed to be remembered visually. And it would be good, I thought, as he had placed very low priority and interest in arts and culture. There may be a case to have a painting of him, for when he was alive, he did not sit for a portrait. He had declined that anything be named after him, any building or institution. And I noticed a lot of other Singaporean presidents or important ministers before him all had their portraits painted. At that time, there were a few portrait painters that I knew, really good painters, like Chua Mia Tee. I contacted Chua Mia Tee in 2010 and asked if he still painted portraits. He said no, his eyesight was poor and his attention span was getting shorter. He had stopped painting portraits, and had stopped commissioned portraits completely. So, he was ruled out. Another good painter was Siew Hock Meng. He too could not. He did his last commissioned work painting the portrait of the founder of Genting, Tan Sri Lim Goh Tong."

He leans back, looks at me and laughs. "So many good Singaporean artists are getting old. So, I went to this Indonesian artist whom I thought was very suitable. From time to time, I visited the Red Sea Gallery at Dempsey. I talked to the owner Chris Churcher. He suggested Syaiful Rachman. His signature portraits are composed of hundreds, even thousands, of minuscule, faceless human figures. This 'anonymous crowd' approach is not merely a clever contrivance, it also serves as an analogy to the roots of popular culture. That amidst our glorification and idolatry of the powerful, it is easy to forget that it is the power of people that holds them aloft. So, his style of using many small human figures, in a pointillist manner to form the painting of a portrait, is perfect. I thought that would be very appropriate for Lee Kuan Yew, as his whole life was dedicated to the ordinary man. So, I commissioned Syaiful Rachman."

He picks up his mobile phone and scrolls to a red painting of a smiling Lee Kuan Yew, made up of many small human beings. The painting is light and curious, like a jigsaw, as if, given time, every one of the human figures would 'walk out' and the portrait would just be a red background. Its inventive style draws your gaze to it, and it is indeed a suitable piece for a politician. It could be said that a popular politician is only as good as the support he gets from the people he serves. They come together to make him look good, and if they decide to walk, he would literally disappear, amounting to nothing.

"The second painting was done by a Singaporean artist, Boo Sze Yang," he says, his voice light and airy. "The artist actually observed the funeral of Mr Lee in March 2015. He found it rather unusual that over a week of mourning, more than one and a half million Singaporeans turned up to pay their respects. The queue was very, very long. The people came from all walks of life; celebrities stood in line with hawkers, businessmen with housewives. And that week was unusually wet with a lot of rain, particularly in the morning. He painted the occasion by painting a lot of figures, Singaporeans from all walks of life coming to attend the funeral. There was a series of four paintings and I bought two."

He called the first piece *Thank You Lee Kuan Yew*. And the second, *Goodbye Lee Kuan Yew*.

"Cheong Soo Pieng was a very confident artist who knew exactly where he stood, not just an artist in the Singaporean context. He saw himself internationally as one of the important overseas Chinese artists."

08

Collecting Art, Supporting Artists

Chapter 8

Collecting Art, Supporting Artists

A Star of Nanyang, Cheong Soo Pieng

In 1952, four artists, Liu Kang, Chen Chong Swee, Chen Wen Hsi and Cheong Soo Pieng made a trip to Bali. They were searching for a visual language that would help them express how they felt in their new found home in Southeast Asia. All four artists had been born in China, were graduates of Shanghai's Xinhua Academy of Fine Arts, had moved to Singapore, were associated with Nanyang Academy of Fine Arts (NAFA), and were familiar with the teachings of the Paris School of Art. The Bali trip turned out to be historic, one of the most important journeys made by artists out of Singapore. On their return, an exhibition was held, and the paintings on show became symbolic representations of the 'Nanyang' style, which became an important expression of art that was influenced by both West and East, yet uniquely tropical and Southeast Asian. The synthesis of the artistic techniques was not bound by mediums, and Nanyang artists produced both ink and oil works.

Nanyang in Chinese means 'Southern Ocean', a term used to refer to Southeast Asia from the geographical perspective of China. Nanyang art is seen as a significant period in Singapore's art history, as it demonstrates some of the early conscious attempts by artists based in Singapore to generate a local art discourse and identity. It coincided with a political awakening sweeping across the colonised world after the war. In 1959, Singapore achieved self-government status. In the creative circles, it was also a period when architects and artists were active in wanting to be part of the nascent nation-building process, wanting to give an identity to Singapore through the expressions of their work.

"I was a young architect coming back from Melbourne University in 1962." Seow Chuan's eyes show he is deep in thought; this was an important part of the political history of Singapore he wanted to recall specifically. "I had left when Singapore was a British Colony. I came back, and the year after, Singapore became part of Malaysia; three years later Singapore became an independent republic. I was captivated and moved by this notion that we were a new nation. As my career as an architect began, I felt very much part of the nation-building process. Also, as someone interested in art, I witnessed local artists here exploring and trying to find a new form of expression arising from their new reality."

This morning, I am quietly excited. I have come to a critical part of the book, getting into the story of an important artist and an equally important collector. Cheong Soo Pieng is acknowledged by art historians and collectors alike to be the most important pioneer artist of Singapore, one that pushed artistic boundaries and was regarded as a bold innovator. Koh Seow Chuan, an architect, is probably the most illustrious collector of modern and contemporary Singaporean and Southeast Asian artists. How these two met and forged an artist-collector relationship is a story that many in the art world are interested in, yet it is one that has not been told. As usual, his wife Wen Gin has made a strong coffee for me, and I am all ready to move the clock back to the 1960s.

In 1967, Seow Chuan was appointed to the Stamp Advisory Committee by the Minister of Communications and Transport, Yong Nyuk Lin. In 1969, the committee began to consider the works of artists for postage stamps, on Seow Chuan's recommendation, and that was when Cheong Soo Pieng and Koh Seow Chuan first met. "We had identified one of Cheong Soo Pieng's paintings, an oil painting of the Singapore River, as the visual for the stamp. Artist Choy Weng Yang was also in the committee so he was also present along with the Minister." Seow Chuan pauses — he seems to be ordering the sequence of the meeting before describing the artist. "I remember Cheong Soo Pieng walking into the meeting. His face was practically expressionless. The artist was a man of few words. He was probably 40 then, but was already seen as one of the most outstanding artists among the pioneers. Together with Georgette Chen, he had been interviewed by British art historian and collector Michael Sullivan. Sullivan considered him to be the most imaginative and innovative Chinese artist with enormous influence on the younger artists. And by the late 60s and early 70s, his works were selling well. At the meeting, I saw a confident artist, someone who knew his mind. While he was honoured that his painting had been selected, he wanted the government to buy the painting from him, that, to him, was the real honour, not him donating it to the government."

Seow Chuan takes a sip of tea. Wen Gin can tell from my face that I am all ears. Even today, an artist would probably not insist that the government buy their art, but this was in the 1960s. Then or now, most might happily donate their artworks. His art was selling well, he did not need the money. But to him, it was probably the principle, that artists, like any other occupation in Singapore, were professionals that needed to be accorded respect.

"The government and the Ministry of Culture had no funds to purchase the art," Seow Chuan continues in an even voice. "And at that time I did not know any wealthy Singaporean who could be a patron, to buy it from him and donate it to the government. The painting was not so expensive, but it was still a lot of money at that time. The meeting ended cordially. In the end, another artist's work was chosen."

"What were your first impressions of him?" I am keen to know Seow Chuan's reaction to this unexpected turn.

"He definitely had his own mind," Seow Chuan replies. "Of course, he felt proud that his painting was selected. But he also wanted the government to buy his art, that, to him, was real recognition. Donation was easy, but pushing to see if the government would buy took guts and conviction. It showed me that he was a very confident artist who knew exactly where he stood. He didn't just see himself as an artist in the Singaporean context, he saw himself internationally as one of the important overseas Chinese artists. He had already come back from Europe, with successful exhibitions in London in 1962, in Munich the same year, then in Oxford in 1963. There was no Cultural Medallion then, but in 1962 he was awarded the Meritorious Service Medal, a rare and prestigious honour, rarer than the Cultural Medallion, which was initiated in the late 1970s."

Seow Chuan thinks they connected because each understood the situation of the other. In the early days, the government was biased against both local architects and artists. "He felt I was sincere. As an architect, I also knew the difficulties pioneer artists faced in the early years. The playing field was not level and local talents were not recognised by the local authorities, who felt that Singapore did not have great architects and artists. For instance, for big projects, when there was an architecture competition, the government as well as some developers always prescribed that we partnered with a foreign firm to work alongside. I saw artists having the same problem. Because of this position, people who wanted to collect art were influenced by the attitude of decision-makers and institutions. In the early years, the majority of Singaporean artists were Chinese. A lot of the older Chinese tended to collect Chinese art, art by Chinese artists from China. And that continued for a long time."

After his first 'stamp' interaction with the artist, Seow Chuan told himself, when he had more money, he would start to collect art from Soo Pieng. And in 1973, he bought his first Cheong Soo Pieng painting. "The first painting I bought was a very early watercolour done in 1947. It was relatively cheap, so I bought it. Then, I could only afford one. I only bought more much later, especially in the late 1970s and after he passed away in 1983. While he was alive, I was unfortunately very busy with my architecture career, the People's Park Complex, Golden Mile Complex and the massive Marina Square project. Those were the most important years of my career. The time that we did spend together underlined what I thought of him: a quiet, serious man who was confident. He took me seriously because he thought I was sincere. I am a confident architect and I saw in him a confident artist. And although his works sold well and he was popular, he was an under-rated artist; I thought his art could soar much higher. Then he died unexpectedly of a heart attack in 1983."

It was only after his death that Seow Chuan realised how important he had been to the artist, and how much the artist had trusted him. "In the 1980s, his daughter Cheong Leng Guat had a shop in Tanglin Shopping Centre. Leng Guat was the one who had travelled with Soo Pieng most often. Born in 1955, she had travelled to Malaysia and

Indonesia with her father during her teens. Even after her father died, she maintained a close relationship with him spiritually. She would ask to see me at her shop in Tanglin."

In the 1990s, as Seow Chuan began to earn a bit more money, he contemplated collecting Soo Pieng more seriously. The artist was popular, and always had ready buyers, but Leng Guat was cautious about letting her father's works go too quickly. She wanted collectors her father was close to to see the artworks first.

"The real buying relationship started with an oil portrait of a Chinese girl, and she said it would cost a low five-figure sum," Seow Chuan remembers as he lifts his head. "It would be the amount her father would have sold it for. I did not say yes immediately. I couldn't, because I really didn't have the money then. By then, I had started to know other collectors and art galleries and they advised me that the price was fair, given the reputation of the artist and the quality of the portrait. I had not paid that amount for any painting up to that point. I was buying Lim Tze Peng for a lot cheaper, and Lim Tze Peng had always encouraged me to buy Soo Pieng. So eventually, after about nine months, I said yes, I would buy the painting for that amount."

But Seow Chuan knew he alone could not help the artist much, especially against the backdrop of prejudice local collectors had. Leng Guat wanted to sell her father's works, and at a price commensurate with her father's reputation in the art world. She auctioned her father's works in Christie's and Sotheby's, but they did not sell as well as she had hoped; in fact, one or two did not sell at all because of the preference for foreign artists.

"It came to a stage where I said this cannot be, this won't do," says Seow Chuan. "I rustled together a few of my artist friends, collector friends and gallery friends. They were professionals, their eyes were trained, and they knew when to buy, who to buy and what opportunities were out there. Like me, they were impressed by Soo Pieng's works and told me we could buy them together."

With this arrangement, Seow Chuan started to have more confidence, now that he had the support of a group of professionals. On top of his own judgement, he had the knowing eyes of many others. And when he bought the artist's works, he could also exit and sell them when he needed to. "Slowly, I became a conduit, indirectly promoting the artist, benefitting the family." Cheong Leng Guat called him Mr Koh, and Koh Seow Chuan soon became the person who saw Cheong Soo Pieng's art first, who had first right of refusal. Seow Chuan's team began to buy more. That was how the relationship between him and the family started to build.

In the early 1980s, William Hsiong came into the picture. He had retired from oil trading in 1980 with money in his pocket. "I went to Leng Guat and told her I now had a collector partner who would like to acquire her father's artworks," Seow Chuan says with a slight grin. "I could tell she was relieved and she said, if you buy from me, you'd be the one promoting my father's art. I'll sign over all the copyright to you and your partner." He pauses, and when he continues, his words are more deliberate. "She was thinking of her father's legacy. Artists always hold their copyright. If you want to reproduce anything, you have to ask the artists or their families for the rights. When you have the copyright, you don't need their permission — that's the fastest way of promoting an artist. I don't have to go through the red tape of writing and getting approval. Now, with this, I had an express lane from the artist's family. It showed me that the family had absolute trust and confidence in me. Whatever artwork I bought from the artist, copyright of the artwork was given to me. William Hsiong was amazed at the trust the family had in me. To this day, 30 years later, I never, at any moment, misplace that trust."

Today, decades later, Seow Chuan's relationship with the Cheong family continues to be strong. After Leng Guat's passing, the artist's only surviving son continues the contact with him. "Leng Guat's brother continues the tradition of offering me important works by his father."

Quintessential Beauty

Cheong Soo Pieng is considered one of the most innovative and influential Singaporean artists of the 20th century. Having known the artist and now possibly being his biggest collector, how does Seow Chuan see Cheong Soo Pieng's art in relation to the other important pioneer artists like Liu Kang, Georgette Chen or Chen Wen Hsi?

"To me, Georgette Chen is like an institutional artist," Seow Chuan begins thoughtfully. "She painted one way, mainly portraits and still life in oil. She was in Paris for quite some time, and was influenced by the Paris School, so it was predominantly portraits and still life. During Liu Kang's time, there were a lot of people following him. His paintings were always popular with collectors. Chen Wen Hsi was a bit more like Soo Pieng but somewhere in the middle. He also explored abstraction, cubism. He did not only draw his bread-and-butter ink on paper — cranes, gibbons, fish — he also explored doing art in different ways. But unlike his peers, or those who were before or came after him, Soo Pieng was the one who continuously experimented and was a real innovator. He went from realism to abstract realism, abstracting the essence of the real, visualising in abstract images. He was seen as the quintessential Nanyang artist. The elongated limbs of the Balinese women he depicted, their oval eyes and full lips, were seen as the essence of what tropical,

Nanyang art was about. To me, that was the pinnacle of Nanyang feminine beauty. He did not paint what a camera could capture as the image of the object. He started out being very humble, getting to know the place and the people. He sketched and sketched — he sketched a lot. A Malay woman, a Eurasian woman, an Indian man, the man in the street, you could see he respected humanity. He always believed that humans had to live in harmony with nature. No enemies. It was always about being at one with nature. Throughout his life, he never deviated from that. He lived it as if it was the spirit that guided him. His work became very spiritual to me, very human, very modest. Very much from the heart. But he was never still. He experimented and experimented. Many thought they knew him, but they only knew him superficially. They didn't connect the various parts of his craft. They looked at the end product and said, I like this or I like that."

Seow Chuan has many catalogues on the table. Some are enormous, taking up almost half of the coffee table. He picks one, *Soo Pieng: Drawings, A Centenary Reflection.* "Soo Pieng made more than 2,000 drawings in the course of his life's work, from which he produced a large body of major artworks in many expressions." He flips the cover and the first few pages to show how the artist progressed from sketches to artworks. "Soo Pieng was always drawing. By the end of his career, there were large numbers of drawings that were stacked up in both his studio and home. His drawings relayed his fascination with people and his surroundings. Always empathetic, he drew almost everyone he saw and interacted with. The drawings were done in pencil, ballpoint pen, pen, and ink and watercolour. Here is a night watchman… a Chinese woman, a Malay woman, an Indian man, a Eurasian woman. He would invite them to his studio in order to paint them. He could have painted from a photograph, but no. He painted what he thought were the essential features of their beauty. The essence, not the real. So even in realism, he was abstracting. His abstracts became sharper and sharper as he went along until he travelled to London and met the abstract painters themselves. From realism, his works eventually became quite abstract in the 1960s, like Zao Wou-Ki's."

I pick a catalogue with the painting of a woman on the cover, *The Story of Cheong Soo Pieng*. I want to bring Seow Chuan back to the visual expression that Cheong Soo Pieng is known for today, his signature of women in the tropics with elongated limbs, oval eyes and full lips.

"In many ways, Bali was, to him, the quintessential essence of beauty and it influenced him most," he says, as he stands to flip the catalogue, searching for a depiction of what he is describing. "To him, that was the epitome of beauty, pure beauty, natural beauty. Not beauty corrupted by the urban setting where women used cosmetics. He eventually came up with a signature look, women of the tropics with long limbs, big eyes and full lips. You could trace this style even to his paintings in the 1940s, but it evolved and found familiarity in the sisterhood of others and soon this style stayed. To him, that was the essence of beauty. In architecture, it is also important to capture the essence. The best is when it is captured in a few lines, visually simple elements to constitute beauty, not complex ones. Beauty in its essence is very simple and easily appreciated because it's from the heart."

It has been more than four decades since the artist's passing — have views of the artist changed? What do people look for when they look at a Cheong Soo Pieng artwork today? Seow Chuan listens contemplatively, then reaches for a file of newspaper cuttings. A *Straits Times* article dated 30 November 2015, headlined: *Pioneer Singapore artist's work sold for $1.4m*.

"His works have consistently reached and some have crossed the million-dollar mark." Seow Chuan sits back and looks at the article. "This piece, *Balinese Dancer*, some people thought was unusual. It was included in the Christie's auction in 2015 that was dedicated entirely to Singapore art. The work had been shown in a late 1950s art publication. It erased his record set the year before. The only other local artist doing better than Soo Pieng is Georgette Chen, and that's really because of scarcity. Georgette did not produce that many works." He reaches out to his catalogue again and flips to an artwork, *Mother and Child*, 1981. "Why is a Cheong Soo Pieng artwork good, you asked. Composition. They are good because of their compositions. As an architect, composition is very important. For Soo Pieng, that composition is balance, a balance between man and nature, a harmony." His eyes gaze at the painting as if he is conversing with the painted characters.

"Next, his choice of colour." Seow Chuan's voice rises. "When you see a Cheong Soo Pieng painting, you can see it is a Southeast Asian painting. The colours are Southeast Asian, there is an earthy tone, with sharp highlights that surprise. Soo Pieng said nature is very complex, and yet it is also very simple. When you see how he depicted nature, when you see his leaves, for instance, you don't see leaves in their primary green colour. His colours are not bright and sharp, but subdued. It may be mustard green, not strong emerald green. He mixed his colours to attain a tone that is strong but soothing. His blues for example, he would mix a little, so that it is deep blue but also calm and striking, never overpowering or overbearing. And the composition of colours, how he applied colours in various corners of his canvas, was important. He would apply a dash of bright red when he wanted it to be the focal point. He would draw your eyes to it.

In many ways, he was the artist who benefited most from the 1952 trip to Bali, and he got so much out of it that he went back several times, not just to Bali but other parts of Indonesia and Malaya. The success of the 1952 trip triggered many other trips by other groups, like the Ten Men Group. He was the trailblazer. He went to Borneo and Sarawak. He even got Loke Wan Tho, his first patron, to fly people to his studio for him to paint them."

It is way past noon, and Seow Chuan has been talking about Cheong Soo Pieng for almost three hours. He stands, stretches, then sits again. He has more to say, it seems, "A few more points then we can go for lunch. What I want to talk about is how influential he was as a teacher and with younger artists then. During that time, the student-teacher relationship was, as a student you don't know, as a teacher I know and I will teach you, you listen or follow. But he taught his students the guiding principles, and would tell them, this is how I paint, don't copy me. You have in yourselves your own innate ability. You want to develop yourself to the maximum of your ability, so follow your heart. Don't copy the way I paint, copy instead the spirit of how I paint. In other words, when he taught, he strove to inspire his students, not just teach his students."

Soo Pieng started with watercolour, a tough medium, for once you apply it, you can't paint over it. It would take away the life or wet 'smudge' the medium is admired for, so a watercolourist needs to get it right the first time. "I was told, a lot of the students who walked past his studio hoped the door was open, so they could look in and see what he was doing. Many times, they would see him deep in thought, smoking his cigar. In the early years, he smoked quite a lot. He thought deeply and for a long time, until he was absolutely sure what he wanted to paint. When he was happy with the image in his mind, his execution was swift and fast. From what Leng Guat told me, he could paint one or two ink on paper works in one day because the images in his mind were very clear. If it was oil, it would take three to five days to complete one artwork. Leng Guat told me the students liked to observe him to understand his thought process and approach towards painting, which most of them thought was spiritual."

"How many Cheong Soo Pieng artworks do you have now?" I ask, half-expecting him not to answer.

"I had many once," he says. "But I have donated many to institutions, and many are now in the hands of collectors who 'cherry-picked' from my collection. I am happy that I have been a successful conduit in promoting the art of Cheong Soo Pieng."

Fishing by Cheong Soo Pieng.

"I think I am very fortunate to have a collector like Koh Seow Chuan. He has made me want to work even harder."

Lim Tze Peng

09

A Patron's Role

Lim Tze Peng Exhibition at Singapore Art Museum 2003. From left to right: Guest of Honour Minister Lee Boon Yang, Mr and Mrs Lim Tze Peng, Koh Seow Chuan, Koh-Lim Wen Gin, Tommy Koh and Kwok Kian Chow.

Chapter 9

A Patron's Role

The Most Popular Singapore-born Artist: Lim Tze Peng

Koh Seow Chuan was not Cheong Soo Pieng's first patron, Loke Wan Tho was. But he was Lim Tze Peng's first major collector, and, over the course of a decade, was instrumental in the artist gaining prominence, nominating him for the Cultural Medallion which the artist received in 2003 at the age of 82. Today, Lim Tze Peng is 103 and still painting, a unique phenomenon. He is arguably the most popular artist in Singapore, known for his calligraphy and ink landscapes. The story of Lim Tze Peng and Koh Seow Chuan is a story of success in the art world, and how success itself can end a successful collaboration.

"I got to know Lim Tze Peng through Gim Ng of Shenn's Gallery in Ubi Techpark in 1989," Seow Chuan begins slowly. "Even though I don't visit him frequently now like I used to before, he still calls me on the second day of Chinese New Year to wish me well, every year without fail. It shows that deep down he is still grateful for what I did for him in those early years."

Gim Ng had about 30 of Lim Tze Peng's works consigned to him; he knew Seow Chuan had a bigger appetite than that, so he advised the collector to meet the artist directly.

"Lim Tze Peng was in his early 70s when I met him at his house in Lorong G, Telok Kurau," Seow Chuan says with a tinge of nostalgia. "I remember, then, it was a single-storey bungalow. Because the house was old and single-storey, he wanted to rebuild it to make it a more substantial abode. He had a contractor friend who drew him a pair of semi-detached houses and suggested that Tze Peng have it built; he would take one house while the artist took the other. This way, his house would be rebuilt with no cost to the artist. Lim Tze Peng lived in a rented house for one-and-a-half years while his bungalow was being rebuilt into a pair of semi-detached houses. As an architect, I found it to be quite a clever and interesting concept. He was frugal, seeing himself as a poor artist with a family to feed."

Seow Chuan bought Lim Tze Peng's works from Gim Ng and also directly from the artist, and by the early 1990s Seow Chuan had amassed quite a lot of the artist's works. "My wife and I were particularly taken by how he recorded places in Singapore that were disappearing: the kampongs, streets scenes and Chinatown, and of course, the Singapore River."

Wen Gin was an architect herself with the Urban Redevelopment Authority (URA) from 1974, and she spearheaded the development of the city centre and championed the conservation of Singapore's built heritage. Wen Gin rose through the ranks of URA and became the Chief Planner and Deputy CEO from 2001 to 2008. "I will say this," Wen Gin smiles. "After selling our Pearl Bank apartment, the bulk of the earnings went to buying Lim Tze Peng's artworks. I would buy 30 to 40 at one go. I was championing conservation and his works captured a disappearing part of Singapore very well. Not just the shophouses, but the street activities too. When I looked at them, I could feel the streets coming to life. His early works were of that quality. When we were staying at our Pasir Panjang Hill house, all our walls were covered in Lim Tze Peng's works, every wall. That was how fond we were of Lim Tze Peng's art."

In the first exhibition staged for Lim Tze Peng, *Meeting Places in Fleeting Spaces*, Wen Gin and Seow Chuan wrote in a foreword:

> *Painting with great fervour before bulldozers erased our dilapidated shophouses to the ground to give way to Singapore's urban redevelopment, he gives expression to the old as beautiful. He saw in our cityscapes, a charm behind the cracks in the walls and columns, the grime and the dirt. His paintings show us the beauty and simplicity of our rural landscapes. No other Singaporean painter in the past thirty years could have captured this so well, in the medium of Chinese ink, with a distinctly Singaporean touch and spirit.*

Aside from how he was recording the disappearing locales of Singapore, Seow Chuan thought it was important for him to collect art by someone who was part of the Ten Men Art Group. "To me, the Ten Men Art Group represented the heart and soul of Singapore. They were documenting and creating art that reflected the local spirit. At that time, there was a camaraderie amongst the artists — they helped each other and worked as a group. That spirit was important. They were different from those who came back from the West, who were affected by democratic ideas and very individualistic. This group was more communal — they looked out for one another."

By now, in the late 1990s, Seow Chuan was already a board member of the National Heritage Board, and had been the chairman of the Singapore Art Museum. He was a prominent person in the art circle. He also had William Hsiong as an investment partner, and as a team, they were formidable. "I was able to get William to collect stamps too, and he was acquiring stamps through me." Seow Chuan's face breaks into a smile. "I would transfer the money I got from stamps to art. From 1998 onwards, I helped stage more exhibitions for Lim Tze Peng than I did for any other artist, many more than for Cheong Soo Pieng."

The first exhibition was held in June 1998 at Singapore Art Museum (SAM), curated by Bridget Tan; following this was a joint donation in 2003 to SAM from the artist and Seow Chuan. "For the exhibition, I loaned SAM all the ink and brush works from my collection. Even though I had started collecting Lim Tze Peng only three years prior, I had a pretty extensive collection. I got Bridget to write the catalogue and I paid for it, and I remember paying for the big reception as well. Even though this was Lim Tze Peng's third exhibition, it was his first in a museum and I wanted it to be a solid event. I wanted him to make an impression. I wanted the exhibition to create an impact."

Kwok Kian Chow, the director of SAM then, told the media that it was the first time a collector had loaned the museum the entire collection of exhibits for a show, and paid for the catalogue and reception as well. "We hope more art collectors can do the same, so that we can have more shows on the works of Singapore's artists at the museum."

"I remember my entire family, four children — three daughters and one son — all being fans of Mr Lim's Chinese ink and brush paintings," Wen Gin says with a joyful voice that carries good memories. "For several years, we would all visit him during Chinese New Year without fail."

While the collector's family felt affection for the artist, the feeling was mutual. In an interview with *The Straits Times*, Lim Tze Peng said, "I think I am very fortunate to have a collector like Mr Koh. He has made me want to work even harder."[1]

---

[1] *The Straits Times*, Monday, 8 June 1998.

And work harder he did. The next big milestone came during 2003. It was a big year for the artist. Seow Chuan had nominated Lim Tze Peng for the Cultural Medallion and he received it that year. It was also the year that SAM received the biggest Lim Tze Peng art donation — 231 works — of which 81 came from the artist and 150 had been donated by Seow Chuan. To acknowledge the gift, SAM held a huge exhibition simply called *Tze Peng*. The exhibition featured 65 works — seven calligraphic works, 20 oil on canvas and 38 ink paintings from the donation. Bridget Tan, curator of the exhibition, was all praise, declaring that the artist had finally found his identity and himself in his art. "Lim today moves with an unparalleled boldness and vigour… Great artists are people who find the way to be themselves in their art, so said famed dancer Margot Fonteyn. It is fitting that in travelling the world to make his mark, to make his art, Lim Tze Peng arrives at perhaps the key destination: himself, in every artwork he produces. With his paintings, we do not just see. We are emboldened to share in his spirit of art."[2]

From the 1990s to the early 2000s, the artist could do no wrong, and his ascension was meteoric. The success of 2003 led Seow Chuan to explore with the artist how he could reach a new level of art, one that built on his history but also one that would depart from it, a real artistic breakthrough. "Success seemed to fuel him to experiment and want to do more. He wasn't young, but he certainly wasn't old as shown by the way he carried on with his work. In fact, he existed only for art. He told me if art was taken away from him, he would have no reason to live. I was impressed by how humble he was, that success hadn't changed him and with how much more he wanted to achieve with his art. Through the years, from 2004 to 2006, we were close and we talked

---

[2] Tze Peng Catalogue, *Destination: Lim Tze Peng* by Bridget Tracy Tan, Page 31

about his art often. I said to him: 'From here on, you mustn't continue to replicate what you have done all your life, don't do the same scenes again and again. Old scenes have disappeared, don't repeat them. When the spirit of the places have already vanished, don't try to capture the places, spiritless. You have the Cultural Medallion; it would be an anti-climax if you just repeated yourself. You must have created a thousand works or more by now, you must be confident now.' He agreed. That was when he experimented with the abstract tree series. He also reconnected with his first medium, oil. With oil, he painted a batch of 40 to 80 paintings. Then he stopped because he felt it was too tedious. For ink, he did smaller paintings, one metre by one metre. Then he went big. He became so inspired and I said, 'That's it! That's what we like to see. You have been newly-inspired; you are born again.' He was capturing art in the abstract realism of the tree, and it proved to be the

most innovative phase of his career."

Seow Chuan staged what would be the most important exhibition for the artist, *Inroads: Lim Tze Peng's New Ink Work* at Art Retreat Museum, at the ground floor of Ubi Techpark in 2008. The exhibition was curated by Teo Han Wue. "It was an exhibition everyone talked about. It showed that overseas Chinese artists were painting differently from the Chinese artists in China. It was a Southeast Asian type of abstract realism, not from the West, not from the East, but from Southeast Asia, which was like what Cheong Soo Pieng was doing before him. His abstract tree series, together with his muddled calligraphy he had invented at the same time, took the art world by storm. They hailed the arrival of a new style in Chinese ink. Kwok Kian Chow said it was such an important exhibition that he invited Professor Fan Di'an, the Director of the National Art Museum of China, to see the works when he was visiting Singapore. It was a visit that would bring the artist's career to yet another level, making him the first Singaporean artist to be invited to exhibit in China."

In 2009, the *Inroads* exhibition was brought to Beijing and Shanghai. The artist's success in China had a big impact on his career. Suddenly, many local galleries started to pursue him, wanting to represent him. He couldn't paint fast enough for the galleries, which began to hold their own mini exhibitions for him. The prices of his works started to climb and he officially got his eldest son to manage the sale of his works.

"When all the galleries descended on him, I knew he had taken off and he didn't need me anymore," Seow Chuan stops, leaning back. "For me, and others like Bridget Tan, Teo Han Wue and Kwok Kian Chow, we had done all we could for the artist. Now the galleries could take over. When he became even more popular after China, his son became more prominent in representing his father's interests. Lim Tze Peng started to sell well. Then two years ago, following the launch of the book you wrote about him, *Soul of Ink*, launched by the Prime Minister, he became even more popular. It was the perfect media story, an artist still painting at 100 years old, embraced by the Prime Minister himself. For a period, every media platform had a story of the 100-year-old artist, the story caught the imagination of the general population in Singapore, and Lim Tze Peng became a star artist. I feel I have achieved my aim of promoting a brilliant Singaporean artist. Therefore, I moved on to other outstanding Singaporean artists who I felt needed my support, and I ended up with someone who was quite literally the opposite of Lim Tze Peng."

In Search of Meaning: The Enigmatic Tang Da Wu

In August 1995, Tang Da Wu approached President Ong Teng Cheong at an art event and asked if he could put on a jacket with the words 'Don't Give Money to the Arts' embroidered on the back. With the President's consent, Tang proceeded to put on his jacket before passing the President a handwritten note with the words, "I am an artist. I am important."[3]

Unknown to the President and everyone else there, Da Wu was staging a piece of performance art, engaging the President as a 'collaborator'. This takes on more significance because unscripted performance art had been discouraged in Singapore following Josef Ng's act of snipping his pubic hair at a public event in 1994, and the National Arts Council (NAC) started a no-funding rule on performance art as a result. As Eugene Tan noted later in his article on the work, "By implicating the President in a performance that had not been permitted, Tang demonstrated an artist's ingenuity in circumventing restrictions on his artistic expression and highlighted the significance of art that could not be readily commoditised."[4]

Unlike Lim Tze Peng, who focuses on painting, Tang Da Wu works in a variety of mediums, including drawing, painting, sculpture, installation and performance art. Also, unlike the centenarian who was self-taught, Da Wu studied in the United Kingdom, majoring in sculpture. He graduated with a BA in Fine Arts with first-class honours from Birmingham Polytechnic in 1974. In 1979 he returned to England for further studies, earning a Master of Fine Arts from Goldsmiths'

---

[3] "Performing Uninvited: Tang Da Wu" and "Don't Give Money to the Arts" by Goh Wei Hao, posted on 28 Jul 2020, National Gallery Singapore.

[4] "Tang Da Wu's Audacious Performance 'Don't Give Money to the Arts" by Eugene Tan, *FRIEZE* 200th issue.

College, University of London in 1984, and later a doctorate in 1988.

Also in 1988, when he returned to Singapore, Da Wu founded *The Artist Village*, the first art colony to be established in Singapore. It aimed to encourage artists to create experimental art. Members of the Village were among the first contemporary artists in Singapore, and also among the first to begin practising installation art and performance art. T K Sabapathy noted, "The Village was a beacon, and Da Wu both a catalyst and mentor."[5]

Da Wu is also known to use art to express his concern for environmental and social issues. His work, *They Poach the Rhino, Chop Off his Horn and Make This Drink* in 1989 was one of the earliest works of art here to raise awareness of animal abuse. In 1991, *Tiger's Whip*, also known as, *I Want My Penis Back,* consisted of ten life-sized tigers made from wire mesh covered in white linen. Da Wu, wearing a sleeveless white garment, performed amidst them as poacher, tiger, and man consuming the tiger's penis. This installation finally evolved through talks and seminars, into a single tiger pouncing on a rocking chair, with a trail of red fabric akin to a stream of blood.

"I collected Da Wu relatively late in the artist's career," Seow Chuan reflects. His face seems fascinated by a particular memory of the artist. "He was, of course, not mainstream like Tze Peng. If 80 to 85% of the art public is with Tze Peng, Da Wu's is probably 10 to 15%. But he was the darling of the museum circle — curators love him. Outspoken and unorthodox in his methodology, the path of his work has been crucial to the way visual art has developed in Singapore. He pioneered a new way of expression that had not been seen in Singapore or Southeast Asia throughout the 1980s and 1990s, with bold cutting-edge

---

[5] Sabapathy, T. K. (2023). Contemporary Art in Singapore: An Introduction. In J. Say, & Y. J. Seng, *Histories, Practices, Interventions* (pp. 62-71). Singapore: World Scientific.

expressions of street performances, installations made of daily objects, collaboration with the audience, and workshops with children. A true pioneer for the contemporary art scene. I had been watching and monitoring him and his type of artistic expressions, and wondered if what he did suited what I wanted to collect. To be quite honest, I was not attracted by his early works, and while I appreciated his performance art, it wasn't something I would 'collect'. When I collect, my perspective is long-term."

Way back in the late 1980s and 1990s, there was a lull in property development, and work at DP Architects was slow. Seow Chuan used this time to do more research on Da Wu's art. And that was when the Bumiputra series caught his eye.

While he is often seen as a conceptual artist, Da Wu has always considered painting as a focus of his practice, credited for influencing a shift back to figurativism in Singapore in the late 1980s. 'Bumiputra' is Malay for 'son of the soil', or the 'original inhabitant'. These are his portraits in Chinese ink of the residents of Hougang, a northern Singaporean suburb which was transformed from a pig-farming village into a 'new town' of high-rise apartments and shopping malls in the 1980s. This series continued Da Wu's interest in the relationship between people and the environment. The paintings also convey his emphasis on spontaneity and improvisation. The paper must have been damp when he applied the ink, leading to 'bleeding' and 'staining'. The resulting effect is a suggestive portrayal of his subjects, just the essence or spirit of his subjects.[6]

"What the series represents resonated with me very much. Over the years I have collected slightly more than a hundred of Da Wu's works,

---

6 TANG Da Wu; Bumiputra series by Russell Storer GAGOMA Collection. Queensland Art Gallery, Gallery of Modern Art.

and 60 of them are part of this series." He lifts his mobile phone towards me to show me images of Da Wu's ink portraits, which are dramatic and stunning. As opposed to Lim Tze Peng, who emphasises a visual approach to art, Da Wu's is an intellectual approach. While Lim Tze Peng seeks visual breakthrough experimenting with ink, Da Wu on the other hand, is grappling with questions of existence. "Yes, I became attracted to his work because of that. That spiritual or intellectual search for the meaning of life." Seow Chuan's voice is emphatic. "Although he is steeped in Chinese language and culture, this search for me has a western premise, and I was both surprised and intrigued. The path Da Wu embarks on is this intellectual direction with art, a path that is disciplined and occasionally lofty. He is a visionary at heart, he has certain beliefs and he lives them out. He also introduced me to his son, whose art is related to sound. Very deep. But these esoteric approaches don't go very far in Singapore. When you choose this path in art, you will have a smaller but probably more dedicated following. And when they buy his art, they are also willing to pay a bit more."

Between 2008 and 2015, Seow Chuan and his wife let go of their Lim Tze Peng artworks to promote other Singaporean artists. It coincided with a newfound interest in Da Wu. "From a very popular artist, I moved on to an intellectual one, whose approach was moral and uncompromising. Collectors Linda Neo and Albert Lim followed me."

The National Gallery Singapore opened in 2015, and Da Wu would visit Seow Chuan either at his DP Architects office or at his Gallery office. Unlike Lim Tze Peng who has his son or the galleries to sell his works, Da Wu's approach is distinctly different given the esoteric nature of his works. "Because his base is much smaller, he cultivates his clients personally. He would visit me in my office now and then. Sometimes he would come carrying a big painting without me asking for it and say 'You may want to consider this.' He was willing to leave the artwork in my office for three to six months. I started to acquire his art that way. Big paintings. He came to my office and showed me the *Heroes of Singapore Art*, his unique portraits of Liu Kang, Chen Wen Hsi, Georgette Chen, Cheong Soo Pieng and Lim Tze Peng. I bought that series in 2008 and 2009."

Not many people know it, but Da Wu did not accept a nomination once for the Cultural Medallion. Da Wu was the recipient of the Visual Arts Award from the Arts Council of Great Britain in 1978, as well as the Artist Award from the Greater London Arts Council in 1983. In 1999, he was awarded the 10th Fukuoka Asian Culture Prize in Arts and Culture.[7] "I suggested that I would nominate him for the Cultural Medallion, but he told me not to, that he had already refused to accept a nomination once. He did not tell me the reason why he rejected the nomination; I don't know the exact date because I was not involved in it. The incident just showed me how different he was from the other artists in Singapore. He wasn't looking for medals and accolades. Instead, his aim in his art life is to use art to further political and social causes. His aversion to the local authorities and establishment stems from his belief that the local government does not understand art, that their support for art is cursory, across the board, with no real understanding of what is truly needed in the art ecosystem. He did not even want to talk to any government officials except in an exhibition at LaSalle, which was an academic institution. Lawrence Wong was the Guest of Honour. I told him: 'You must come,' and that was the only time he came to talk to Lawrence Wong. He was wearing a T-shirt that said 'Don't Give Money to the Arts'."

[7] Tang Da Wu | The Guggenheim Museums and Foundation, https://www.guggenheim.org.

One is reminded of the jacket he wore in 1995, 'Don't Give Money to the Arts', and the paper he handed to President Ong Teng Cheong with the text, 'I am an artist. I am important.'

There are many other great Singaporean artists that Seow Chuan supports: Wong Keen, Koeh Sia Yong, Zhuang Shengtao, Wong Shih Yaw, Ho Chee Lick, Boo Sze Yang and Yeo Shih Yun, to name a few.

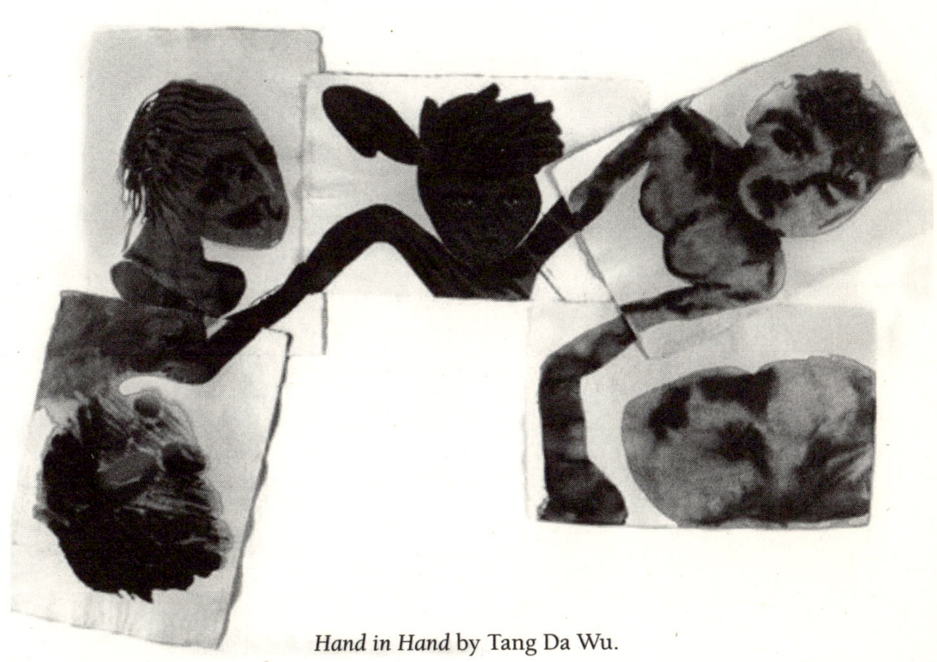

Hand in Hand by Tang Da Wu.

"Stamps gave Seow Chuan that discipline from a young age. So, his approach to stamps led him to the same approach in collecting art, collecting with knowledge."

Melvin Poh

"Seow Chuan has this wealth of information and has access to so many sources of information. So curious, generous and open minded."

Diana Tay

"Seow Chuan told us, if local collectors don't collect works by local artists, the local art scene would never stand a chance against foreign art. There was already bias against local art, he likened it to colonial attitude, thinking only foreign was good."

Linda Neo and Albert Lim

10

The Support He Did Not Make Public

Interviews with Melvin Poh, Diana Tay, Linda Neo and Albert Lim

From left: Linda Neo, Diana Tay, Albert Lim and Melvin Poh.

Chapter 10

The Support He Did Not Make Public

Melvin Poh

I had messaged Melvin earlier to meet for a chat on Seow Chuan. Although they are 30 years apart in age, both are eminent art collectors and each looks at the other with admiration and respect.

Is 9.30 too early, I asked.

I play tennis at seven in the morning, so early is fine with me, he replied. *Can be over breakfast too, your favourite duck noodles.*

Might be a bit noisy, but I enjoy interviewing over a casual meal. *Let's do that, duck noodles at Rocovo, Goldhill. Park at my place and we'll walk across the road,* I said.

9.30am. Melvin arrives in a stately white Bentley; the car number plate is an auspicious EZ 383 Z. For someone who is only 51, he has done very well for himself. A real estate developer and entrepreneur, he only started collecting art a few years ago. But in a short span of time, he has become a collector everyone in the art community looks up to, one of the few English-educated Singaporeans with an interest in collecting Chinese paintings and calligraphy.

"Before I met Koh Seow Chuan formally, I had already known him to be an art collector of considerable means and foresight. Also, my wife and I started working at the Urban Redevelopment Authority, so we knew his wife, Wen Gin. And being in real estate, it was hard not to know the founder of DP Architects and the many prominent buildings he was involved in." Melvin is enjoying the duck noodles, and I am glad this very well-to-do art collector has remained humble and approachable. While he may be used to fancy restaurant food, he has not lost his taste for good hawker fare. "I met Seow Chuan formally in April 2017, at Helutrans, where he keeps most of his art. He set up 35 of Lim Tze Peng's artworks, some of which were huge, very large or monumental works, 5m long by 2.5m wide. I was keen to acquire a good art collection that suited me and my wife. This Lim Tze Peng collection appeared to be an attractive opportunity."

The morning sun inches into *Rocovo*, and I feel the humidity rising. Although it is only April, it feels like a mid-year heat. My T-shirt has started to stick to my skin, and I am beginning to feel uncomfortable. Melvin, in a turquoise T-shirt, is composed, and the heat and humidity do not seem to affect him at all. He continues to enjoy the noodles while talking about the collector he admires. "It was the first time I had seen so many pieces of art of considerable value, and I had asked my wife to come along. That was the start of my journey as a collector, and it began with Koh Seow Chuan parting with some of his Lim Tze Peng artworks."

If there is one word to describe Seow Chuan as a collector, what word would it be? Melvin looks down, thinking. "Singapore-centric, is that one or two words?" he laughs. "And he collects Singaporean artists way before they become famous or before they make it big. In other words, he has an eye for potential; he can suss out a good artist.

He was Cheong Soo Pieng's patron, and also Lim Tze Peng's patron, and now these artists are a big part of Singapore's art history. And he supported them earlier on in their careers. When he decides to support, he supports big, he buys in huge quantities. That's part of his character, that he supports an artist in a very big way."

Even though he wants to 'pass the baton' over to Melvin, Seow Chuan still continues to collect today, but he collects to ensure that good artists stay as artists, that they continue to be a part of the art ecosystem. "Most young artists find it tough in the Singaporean art market, especially those without a name." Melvin has finished the duck noodles and is now nursing a cup of *teh C kosong*. "Seow Chuan buys their works, keeps them, so that they can continue to create. With some artists, he even gives them allowances, and tells them they can pay him later in kind, with their art. You see, if there was no financial support, some of these artists would give up. So, while he has a lot of known artists in his collection, what is not known is that he has a lot of unknown artists too. So, that's the big part about him. And he does it quietly. Only close friends know this part of him. In that way he is not only a good collector, he is also a noble one. I am an art collector too, but I have not reached his level. Most collectors collect art from artists who are already established, or at least are quite established. His is almost an incubator approach — holistic, long-term. He looks at the artists, Singaporean artists, and as long as they have potential, he would want to support them."

Melvin rests his face on his raised hands. "Stamps," he says with a grin. "I heard from the grapevine that he sold one of his stamp collections for half a million in the 1970s. That was a princely sum, a lot of money at that time. Even if the sale wasn't true, we know he was an outstanding, renowned stamp collector. Let's bring ourselves back to the 1970s. There was no internet. To be that renowned a stamp collector, you needed to be a great researcher as well, and I know for a fact that he places a lot of importance on knowledge. Where did he get his knowledge, how did he do his research? In the 70s, the libraries in Singapore were limited. He probably had an extensive network of friends he exchanged knowledge with, and he probably went overseas to plough through all the information in the libraries abroad. I think this method and discipline made him who he was and who he has become. His method or approach was and is knowledge-focused, and as at every step of the way it is knowledge that propels him on. Stamps gave him that discipline from a young age. So, his approach to stamps led him to the same approach in collecting art, collecting with knowledge. Stamps are small pictures, he said. So, this is consistent with what I have always said about him, he is measured. He doesn't just do, he thinks first before he makes his moves. He is the opposite of loud, showy and egoistic architects, and we know there are many of those around."

The humidity has reached an uncomfortable level, and I feel a need to move to an air-conditioned place now. "There is a quieter coffee shop around the corner, just 50 metres away. A no-frills neighbourhood café, *The Clueless Goat*."

"Really, clueless goat," he laughs.

The café has been around since 2015. I like it because it is unpretentious, welcoming and comfortable. Zak, one of the founders, told me the name *The Clueless Goat* was inspired by an ancient story of a goat-herder in Ethiopia, where one of his herds accidentally consumed coffee berries instead of grass. The herder thought he might also experiment and discovered the 'buzz' of coffee from this 'clueless discovery'. With it, the founders created a name that is unique and memorable, and a great conversation-starter with their patrons.

I enjoy *Rocovo* in T-shirt and shorts, but today I am wearing trousers. The cool air in *The Clueless Goat* makes it a most welcome change of environment. "What would we do without air-conditioning in Singapore?" I ask rhetorically. I order two flat whites and we settle down into our new air-conditioned cosiness.

"Art collecting can be very expensive," Melvin's voice resumes in his signature storytelling tone. "It is not something everyone can get into. And even if you have the means, there are other factors. Do you collect with knowledge? Seow Chuan does. And that's important because collecting, serious collecting, can get into millions of dollars. You want to be smart about it as it is a form of investment. Then, there is the home environment. Do your wife and family support what you do? Without the support of your spouse to share your passion, there could be disagreements, even fights. There is always an undercurrent of, hey, why are you spending money on this sort of thing? Fortunately for me, I have a very supportive wife. She is always by my side and knows what I like and dislike. And for major pieces, I will seek her opinion, especially when I have to decide between two pieces, which to buy, so an opinion from her is useful and important. And somehow, ladies have a different aesthetic perception, they are more sensitive. I think the spouse is a very important ally for a collector. Seow Chuan does not share everything he collects with Wen Gin, nor consult her on every piece he buys. But he knows he has a supportive spouse he can discuss collecting with, talk matters over with. And occasionally she too buys and collects. Because they share a life and a home, it is important that the wife is happy with what she sees on the walls, and knows how their wealth is invested. And their daughter helps him with the management of his art. So, all in, the family sees collecting not just as a worthwhile pursuit, it has also become a pleasurable one the entire family can enjoy."

Diana Tay

The plan is to meet Seow Chuan for lunch after my session with Melvin.

A message appears around 10.30 am. *Melvin can join us if he is free.* This message gives me a chance to ride in a Bentley for the first time in my life. And the ride from my residence to the National Gallery Singapore is a quiet, almost silent voyage of soft-leathered luxury.

Most people call the *Courtyard* at the National Gallery Seow Chuan's canteen, but, unlike most canteens, he keeps his special bottle of whisky here to be shared with friends on both routine and special occasions. Seow Chuan looks at the young waiter, and smiles. The waiter nods and presently arrives with a bottle of half-full Glenfiddich, single malt. Melvin looks at Seow Chuan and grins. When your host has such noble intentions, you acquiesce. The waiter pours the gold liquid into two short glasses, then places one in front of Melvin and one beside me.

"Cheers," Seow Chuan raises his glass. "Let me introduce my daughter Lin Ai, and art conservator Diana Tay." Lin Ai greets us with a warm smile. Her eyes are friendly. Diana has a bright demeanour, her hair is cropped, and she looks to be in her 30s.

"I met you here the last time." Diana has a clear youthful voice. I feel a flush of embarrassment, for I have no recollection of meeting her. "Seow Chuan said you were writing a book on him."

Perhaps it was a fleeting introduction and nothing else. "You are an art conservator? How refreshing." A young conservator, an unusual career choice.

"You should talk to her, interview her," Seow Chuan suggests, excited. "She went to Melbourne University, my alma mater. She has a PhD in conservation. Linda Neo introduced her to me; she has now done a good body of work on Cheong Soo Pieng, and we are working quite closely together. But let's order lunch first."

Lunch turns out to be a somewhat rushed affair. Seow Chuan needs to leave by 1pm, he says. Melvin excuses himself as he has his own plans for lunch. I decide to enjoy my Hainanese curry chicken rice, Courtyard's specialty, and when the party disperses, I have my own one-on-one chat with Diana.

Most stories begin at the beginning. I will start Diana Tay's story not at the beginning, but when she had to make a career choice. By her late 20s, she had been an assistant conservator at the Heritage Conservation Centre for eight years. She was also a volunteer, a part-time police officer. "I was quite a good police officer," she says with bright-eyed boldness. "They offered to make me an inspector, a full-time one. And the pay was almost double what I was earning then. I was so tempted. I had been an assistant conservator for eight years. I had funded my own masters, and when I came back, I didn't feel progression. I was not promoted. I was told I questioned too much."

Diana pauses. Her mind seems to pull the brakes on talking about her old job, and she decides to let the past stay in the past. When she resumes, her voice carries a fresh excitement. "One day, out of the blue, I received a phone call. Surreptitious call from a private collector. Are you keen to do your PhD in conservation, she asked. I said no, it's half a million dollars. The caller pressed, put the cost aside, she assured, do you want to? I told her I would think about it. It was just two hours after I received the letter from the Police Force to be an inspector. As I said, the pay was so good, but I remember sitting in City Hall, confused. If the inspector offer was so good, why was I not happy? I kept asking myself."

A chance at a PhD in conservation, the highest level anyone could attain in an academic field of study! She admitted to herself that it excited her, but at the same time she was also terrified, who would fund her studies? How would this unravel? Who or what would she be indebted to? Amidst the confusion and excitement, she decided to avail herself to this bizarre option that had miraculously surfaced.

The private collector who had called her was Linda Neo.

"I told her, if you can connect me to someone who would fund me, why not?" Diana allows a wide smile now. "Then the next week, I met Mr Koh Seow Chuan. It was a meeting that changed my life. He would be the person funding my PhD. And he funded me with absolutely no strings attached."

Then, Seow Chuan was the Chairman of the National Gallery Singapore. To pursue a PhD in conservation, a student needed access to a sizable body of works of a reasonably well-known artist. "He told me, 'Don't worry, apply first.' And so, I did. I would meet him at the National Gallery quite a lot. I recall, during my third meeting with him in 2018, not only did he offer to fund me, which was a very generous offer, he also said I could study his collection. At that point I knew all my bases were covered. For my PhD, I proposed my own topic. I needed to make sure I had artworks to study for the next four, five years. I focused on one artist first, Cheong Soo Pieng. I wanted to build a material database. This material database would be useful for authentication. Mr Koh advised me to choose Cheong Soo Pieng because when an artist becomes famous and his works become expensive, there are bound to be fakes. You can be sure there will be questionable works in the market. Mr Koh had good foresight. Initially I had been keen on choosing Chen Cheng Mei, but his advice was to pick Cheong Soo Pieng. And he was right, Cheong Soo Pieng became a much more important artist, and my study on his works would be valuable not just for collectors but also institutions like the National Gallery. Mr Koh not only guided me on what artist I needed to look at, but also the materials available, like books, catalogues. He drove the direction for the research."

The thrust of Diana's PhD research was to collect a hundred data points for a painting. Here, she identifies the artist's technique and the materials the artist used. "If someone wants to forge a painting, it would be almost impossible to meet all these hundred data points. In one work, I would study how the artist folded the canvas, the canvas thread count, thread count per centimetre; these little, little details. Very detailed. We take technical photographs, which allow us to see beyond the painted image. One hundred data points for one painting. But a single painting won't tell us everything. We need to collect a body of information of, say, 60 works of one artist to go deep, deep, deep. With data from 60 works, we can confidently put forth a report identifying a comprehensive pattern or signature characteristics of the artist. For instance, in the late 60s, the artist used lead and titanium in his backgrounds. In the 70s, he did not use lead any more but had moved to zinc. The artist himself would not know these details, the range of information is from the materials he used — only the manufacturers would know. So we study each piece of artwork in a molecular way, microscopically using science. Data cannot lie, it is no longer subjective. Previously when you assessed whether a work was authentic or not, they would tell you if the brushstrokes were typical of the artist for instance. With science, it is no longer about opinion. There is no subjectivity, it is all objective."

When you are the beneficiary of a generous benefactor, you somehow feel responsible for showcasing how you have benefitted. And for Diana, what rubbed off most is Seow Chuan's patriotism and love for Singapore and Singaporean artists. "He has a great relationship with Helutrans and was able to arrange for me to study the artwork there. They gave me a space to study there. I knew it was a great privilege because there were no other students there except me. And it was while studying there that I saw how passionately he supports local artists and how he helps the arts community here. He would tell me, 'You are doing this for Singapore, remember that.' He kept driving that into my head."

Four years in Melbourne, almost two years running her own conservation business, BARC Labs (Beneath Art Research and Conservation), and she is only in her 30s. What's next?

Diana dismisses the question; she wants to talk more about Seow Chuan, or Mr Koh as she respectfully insists on calling him. "When I say Mr Koh is generous," she looks up and swallows a gulp of emotion that has unexpectedly come up, "I mean he truly does not ask for anything in return, and he doesn't make you feel bad if you don't reciprocate. He gives, that's all. That's such a simple thing, yes, simple, but very hard to find these days. For a lot of people, when they give you something, you know they will ask you for something in return later. Not Mr Koh. He gives and he tells me this is for Singapore. He always reminds me that whatever I am doing, it's for Singapore. It's not for him. Generous. And very curious. His mind is always curious. I really admire that. He wants to know what is beyond the painting, beyond what our eyes can see. Because he knows I have the means to find out, he asks and asks. I can see in his eyes that he is hungry for the knowledge that I have. He is sometimes more curious than I am. And it becomes a good working relationship as we bounce things off each other. For example, I would tell him something about an artist, and he would come back with so much more information about the artist that would help me in my research. He just has this wealth of information. So, it is good to be exposed to him, as he has access to so many sources of information. So curious, generous and very open-minded. And he is very interested in AI (artificial intelligence). I am young, but I wasn't as interested in AI compared to him. So, somehow, this led to the use of AI in my PhD as well. And that was because of him. He wanted to know how AI could help in our research. With the data we collected, we have more than 700 photos. He was able to collaborate with a data scientist, and he would be able to use AI to build the research in a non-biased way. As humans, we could miss out things because we use our eyes. A computer can do a better job of showing the differences between image A and B. So, I used AI in the last part of my PhD. AI was used especially for technical imaging. What can I say, I am in my 30s, he in his 80s, yet we are working so well together. Just incredible."

Linda Neo and Albert Lim

The doorbell rings at ten, on the dot. Very punctual. I have known them for almost 15 years now, since they commissioned me to write my first book on Lim Tze Peng, *My Kampong My Home*. Over the years, Linda Neo and Albert Lim strike me as a couple who excel in almost everything they do, and that, they also do almost everything as a couple. They have been married for close to four decades, and have collected art for two.

"Hahaha, a common interest and philosophy are important to keep the long journey going," Linda says with mirth.

Indeed, common interest and common philosophy. While travelling the globe on business for their banking and finance careers, they would make time for museums, and soon started collecting Western and Renaissance art. Today, their main focus is Singaporean and Southeast Asian art, and they cite Koh Seow Chuan as an important influence and inspiration.

"We got to know Mr Koh around the time we amassed the kampong paintings of Lim Tze Peng for the *My Kampong My Home* exhibition," Linda remembers. "At that time, there were not so many collectors, and he was already known for his vast collection of Singaporean artists, namely Lim Tze Peng. What amazed us was, even though he was a big collector of Lim Tze Peng's work, he was so excited about the exhibition and asked us for a preview. And when the show opened, we invited him. That was the beginning of our friendship. He told us, if local collectors don't collect local artists, the local art scene would never stand a chance against foreign art. There was already a bias against local art, he likened it to a colonial attitude, thinking only all things foreign were good. We were already starting to collect local artists, but his resolute focus on local artists definitely influenced us."

Today, Linda and Albert are the power couple of art, and they count Singapore's foremost contemporary artists Jane Lee and Tang Da Wu in their famed collection. Other artists include Cheong Soo Pieng, Melissa Tan, Suzann Victor, Hong Zhu An and Han Sai Por. In 2014, Primz Gallery was established as a platform to showcase their vast private collection. People who visit them are not only impressed by the good art, but are also taken by the well thought-out storage behind the gallery. Here, hundreds of large artworks are neatly stacked and stored in professionally designed racks.

Albert pursued an MA in Asian Art Histories at LaSalle College of the Arts in 2017. "He was the oldest student," Linda teases. "But he was determined to study art history, a subject he feels all serious art collectors should pursue. I respect that."

"We used to be *paiseh* (embarrassed) about telling people about the art we owned," Albert looks at Linda with a smile. "But Linda and I now realise we have a part to play in the art ecosystem, so we need to be art advocates. At Primz, I conduct art tours myself, and I feel great satisfaction conducting these tours for people and sharing the art with them. Every time I talk about these works, I feel renewed — it's as if I'm talking about them for the first time. This kind of confidence, I must attribute to Mr Koh's influence. Mr Koh has done a lot for the art scene in Singapore and he encourages us to do the same."

Like Melvin, Linda remembers how Seow Chuan collects, "He calls himself a vacuum cleaner, he sucks up everything. If he likes an artist, he buys up all the art the artist has. A person would walk into the opening of an exhibition and show interest in one or two pieces, only to find out that Mr Koh has bought up the entire show."

Albert says Seow Chuan looks at art in an almost personal way. When he likes an artist, he sees himself as a guardian. He does not see himself buying one or two works, but several, enough to have an exhibition for the artist if he wants to push the artist's career further. "What we learned from him is to believe in yourself, which is what he always tells us. It is because he believes in himself that he is bold, and he takes risks in art. In the early days, taking risks in art was almost unheard of. The result of taking risks was that the artists benefited. Let's take Cheong Soo Pieng as an example. Seow Chuan really believed in the artist. He was like the guardian, when people heard that Koh Seow Chuan was buying Cheong Soo Pieng, they felt good because they had the confidence that he would continue to buy and support the artist. So, they too came in and bought his works. We collected Soo Pieng that way, because of him. In the same way, when we saw Jane Lee, and we were convinced that she was a good artist, so we bought and bought her works."

Linda and Albert cite sports, especially swimming, as a key determinant in Seow Chuan's personality, affecting how he approaches collecting. "He is very focused and very competitive," says Linda. "Because of his background in sports, he is not emotional and doesn't allow emotions to get in the way, or get the better of him. While he is creative, he is also structured. You can be an architect, but a good architect needs to be a good administrator as well. This combination of right and left brain, if you like, saw him through DP Architects for more than 50 years. When he decided to support Cheong Soo Pieng, both his creative and administrative sides came together, and he became exceedingly successful in promoting Soo Pieng. I call him an instinctive man and a risk-taker, like a good businessman. He brought the art of business into art. He buys, and he allows aspiring art collectors to 'cherry pick' from his vast art collection. Most artists do not like that their collectors sell their art. But that is unrealistic and also wrong. Buying and parting to collectors who value them show that the artist is in demand. If we don't popularise the artist's works by sharing with other collectors, how are artists going to survive, how can the art ecosystem thrive? Mr Koh is not apologetic in the way he manages his art collection, and I think it is absolutely crucial for a healthy art scene. So, behind the scenes, Mr Koh does many good things for the arts."

Cultural leadership is rare in Singapore. Being a successful architect, and having started collecting young, first stamps, then art, Seow Chuan became an informed and respected cultural personality. By the time he retired from DP Architects, the government saw in him an experienced pair of hands they could go to for many purposes regarding culture. But he was smart to stay independent, knowing that only by being independent would he continue to be useful and respected.

Another aspect of cultural leadership is succession planning. He applied what he practised in DP Architects to the area of culture. Seow Chuan knows what he has done for the art scene in Singapore. But he is also constantly on the lookout for younger, able and well-intending collectors to succeed him. "He has built an ecosystem with people like Melvin and us," Linda asserts. "He encourages us, involves us, and influences us, and in turn we have cultivated a lot of collectors along the way. Since his retirement, he has spent time sitting with people, talking to people about art tirelessly. So, in the two decades since his retirement, he has imparted a lot of experience and knowledge. Invaluable."

"It has been a long journey and a worthwhile one for all of us. We remember your guiding hand in the making of the Gallery. Thank you for being an important part of this project and for encouraging me to grasp the baton you passed on to me."

Hsieh Fu Hua

11

National Gallery Singapore

TO COURT NO.

National Gallery International Design Competition jury panel, with Ministers, in 2006.

Chapter 11

National Gallery Singapore

A Pinnacle of Singapore Art

Seow Chuan is hesitant, and his index finger rests tentatively on his lips. "It is a project I look back on with mixed feelings," he looks at me and breaks into a grudging smile. This is his reluctant 'assessment' of his own role as Deputy Chairman of the National Gallery Singapore Project Steering Committee from 2005 to 2011, Chairman of the Executive Committee for the Development of the National Gallery Singapore from 2007 to 2015, and as Founding Chairman of the National Gallery Singapore from 2009 to 2013. "I had officially retired from DP Architects and was privileged enough to end my architecture career on a high in 2005. These were two of Singapore's most historic monuments, the City Hall, or the Municipal Building as it was first known, and the former Supreme Court building, to be repurposed architecturally into a grand art institution. All eyes would be on what happened to these two buildings. Did I want this burden at this stage of my life? Or should I pursue more personal projects? In the end, of course my sense of duty to the country overrode my doubts. But I went into this role with both my eyes wide open."

At the heart of Singapore's Civic District, overlooking the wide expanse of the Padang, lies City Hall and the former Supreme Court buildings. Completed in 1929 and 1939 respectively, these were, for many years, the frontispieces of the city. Long before Singapore's iconic skyscrapers came to dominate the skyline, this was the view that greeted visitors and played host to significant moments for the nation.

The Civic District, from which modern Singapore sprung, was laid down in accordance with Sir Stamford Raffles' town plan in 1822, shortly after he first established a trading post on the island in 1819. Located at the north bank of the Singapore River, the Civic District was the administrative engine of the British colonial government.

Prior to the City Hall and the Supreme Court buildings, the site had been occupied by three private bungalows, and they were converted into hotels by the mid-19th Century. In 1920, the Municipal Council bought over the land, and in 1926 the two bungalows were torn down to make way for the new Municipal Building, giving it the prime vantage point in front of the Padang.

At the National Day Rally speech on 21 August 2005, Prime Minister Lee Hsien Loong mentioned the government's plan to convert the former Supreme Court building and City Hall into a new national gallery. A year later, on 2 September 2006, Dr Lee Boon Yang, Minister for Information, Communications and the Arts, officially announced the setting up of the National Gallery Singapore during the Singapore Biennale.

So, the National Gallery Singapore, one of the largest visual arts institutions in the region, was a much anticipated addition to Singapore's cultural landscape when it opened in 2015. It had been a decade in the making. The Gallery was the first museum of its kind dedicated to the research and exhibition of Singaporean and Southeast Asian art. Its ambition was to showcase some of the best visual art from the region, host international art exhibitions and strengthen Singapore's position as a regional and international centre for the visual arts.

"In November 2004, I retired from DP Architects," Seow Chuan looks at me from across the table in his living room. On the table is a square book, *The Making of National Gallery Singapore*. "In 2006, I was approached by the government to be the Chairman of the Executive Committee National Gallery Singapore. Balaji Sadasivan, then the Minister of State, Ministry of Information, Communications and the Arts wanted to provide me a fee for my role. I was cautious about being paid. If I served this role as a service to the country, national service, if you like, I would have more independence, and I wouldn't have to toe the line if I disagreed with any official position. To this day I am glad I stuck to my gut feeling, because those years as Chairman of the Executive Committee proved to be professionally the most challenging in my life. The building of the Gallery actually used every aspect of my architectural knowledge and experience. I had to bring everything I knew to the table, and I am glad I could do this for Singapore, from the tender process, the selection of the architects and contractors, to the need for strategic negotiations, cost control and delivering on time, at every stage of the construction. It was a Herculean task and I am glad we delivered. I am talking about the hardware, how we converted the City Hall and the Supreme Court into what we now called the National Gallery Singapore. The software, the artworks themselves, that was a different story."

CPG Consultants had given a rough estimate on how much it would cost to restore and convert the two historical monuments into an art institution. But Seow Chuan did not take things at face value, his years as a collector of stamps and art, and his experience at DP Architects had taught him to arm himself with knowledge, crucial knowledge, first. By the time he was done with his 'investigations', his team presented to Cabinet a cost estimate that was nearly double the original estimate. And he was glad he 'investigated'.

When the Gallery finally opened its doors to the public in 2015, everyone was wowed and swept away by the majesty of the transformation. Singapore finally had an art destination Singaporeans and foreigners wanted to visit. Singapore and Southeast Asian art had a real 'home'. The story of the National Gallery Singapore was a Cinderella story. Few knew about the inherent issues associated with the two buildings, and why the bill added up to a whopping amount.

"It was a large expenditure," Seow Chuan jerks his head up, as if the information weighs heavy on his mind. "There were untold expectations. Almost everyone involved in the arts, intimately or remotely, in Singapore or outside, wanted to be a part of it. Of course, you can understand why. Housed in City Hall and the former Supreme Court, these were two national monuments that tell many stories of our journey as a nation, including the defining chapters in our history."

I was an employee, the Director of Media and Marketing, before it opened. When I walked through the City Hall Chamber, I knew it was where the Japanese surrendered after the Second World War, followed by the swearing in of Singapore's first Prime Minister, Mr Lee Kuan Yew, and members of the first Cabinet in 1959. When I walked out and looked at the Padang, I was reminded that it was on these steps of City Hall that Mr Lee announced the independence of Singapore.

The restoration team had carefully preserved these spaces, including details such as the wooden panelling in the four original courtrooms of the former Supreme Court. It is easy to be caught up in the grandeur, like how City Hall is described in *The Making of National Gallery Singapore*:

From the grand entrance plinth 14 feet above ground level, 18 three-storey-high fluted Corinthian columns rose magnificently, topped by a wide cornice and a 10-foot-high parapet. Corner pavilions completed the façade at both ends, and a central projecting balcony behind the columns acted as a recessed porch for the heavy bronze entrance doors beneath. The front and side elevation of the building were clad with white artificial granite, also known as Shanghai plaster, which set off the design of the steel casement windows and ornamental cast iron balustrades between the columns.[1]

"In Singapore, the British government embarked on a nationwide building programme that saw the completion of many important civic buildings, including the City Hall or Municipal Building in 1929 and the Supreme Court in 1939," Seow Chuan begins slowly. "Yet the political and economic realities at that time were bleak — Singapore was just starting to recover from the Great Depression and tensions in Europe were building up in anticipation of the next war, so the colonial government could hardly afford to be extravagant in its spending. In fact, behind the imposing, exterior grandeur were really two buildings built 'on the cheap' in the 1920s and 1930s. The soil condition of the site would pose a big problem for both the buildings; the restoration would require massive rebuilding, including relooking at how to put in a solid foundation."

The architects, Alexander Gordon and Samuel Douglas Meadows, opted to design the main façade in the neoclassical style, conveying the power and dignity of the Empire through its imposing scale, symmetry and harmonious proportions. While the design of the Municipal Building was expressed in a neoclassical manner, the methods employed in the planning and construction of the building were actually 'modern', driven primarily

[1] *The Making of National Gallery Singapore* by Pauline Ang, National Gallery Singapore.

by pragmatic and economic considerations. While the exterior of the building was designed to project the British Empire's grandeur and power, the floor-to-floor heights of the four-storey structure behind the façade were kept modest and rudimentary. For example, natural stone, a far more expensive construction material, was not used. The modern concept of cladding, in which the finished material was distinct from the building structure, was introduced through the use of Shanghai plaster. Despite the poor soil conditions on the site, the four-storey structure did not have a piled foundation, but was instead supported on shallow spread footings, with a concrete raft under the foundations of the external walls.[2]

Construction of the Supreme Court Building commenced in 1937, eight years after the completion of its neighbour. "It was designed by the Chief Architect of the Public Works Department, Frank Dorrington Ward," says Seow Chuan. "Again, much of the emphasis was given to the design of the building's exterior, which was seen as an important symbol of British power and authority."

Unlike the Old Bailey Courthouse, which it sought to emulate, the Supreme Courthouse building had to be built within a limited budget. No attempt was made, for instance, to provide the usual marble panelling, flooring and decoration. Attention was placed on the more important spaces at the front of the building which featured high ceilings, larger volumes, more refined finishes and ornamentation for maximum visual impact, while the less visible spaces at the back of the building, in sharp contrast, were treated in a utilitarian manner, characterised by small, labyrinthine rooms with low ceilings. One of the most recognisable features of the Supreme Court building would be the main copper dome that overlooked the Padang. Although the dome was designed with St. Paul's Cathedral in mind, it was

---

2 *The Making of National Gallery Singapore* by Pauline Ang, National Gallery Singapore.

in fact 'all exterior', supported internally by large steel trusses and accessible only by a narrow spiral staircase. As with the Municipal Building, the architects took a functional and practical approach in the planning and design of the interiors. Despite the steel shortage, the Supreme Court was one of the few buildings in Singapore that was completely built with structural steel; fabricated and shipped from Britain. But before the steel structure could be erected, the engineers had to deal with the problem of unsuitable ground conditions on the site. This consisted of a non-uniform mixture of sand and mud, below which was a hard clay stratum with varying depth of 40 to 90 feet. In order to support the 40,000-ton building, the engineers designed a piled foundation that was driven through the sand and mud into the hard clay. The Supreme Court building was eventually completed at a cost of $1.75 million, two years after the construction commenced on site.[3]

In recognition of their architectural and historical significance, the City Hall and former Supreme Court buildings were gazetted as national monuments on 14 February 1992. "The Urban Redevelopment Authority (URA) and the Singapore Tourism Board (STB) felt that the two buildings could not be left vacant for too long. They had to be restored and reused for something," Seow Chuan recalls. "They even considered turning them into hotels and various other tourism related uses. Eventually the government thought it would make more sense for it to be reused for such an institution, as the buildings were elegant in the British neoclassical style, therefore it should be reused for something related to culture and the arts. The common assumption then was, they were solid buildings erected by the British."

Seow Chuan had his suspicions when he walked around the

---

[3] *The Making of National Gallery Singapore* by Pauline Ang, National Gallery Singapore.

buildings, "I started with an open mind," he stares into the distance. "I was dealing with old buildings, yes, with historical significance. So, the first thing I did was to investigate, to get the background, information and knowledge regarding the buildings, and the site. Before you start, you have to get accurate information to even begin. That was a discipline I cultivated from young, through stamp collecting. Knowledge must come first."

His suspicions would eventually double the cost of the original estimate. As the Chairman of the Executive Committee, he knew his work was cut out for him, he needed a watertight case to prove to the authorities that they needed to spend that money. And proof meant scientific investigations of the building structures and the soil the buildings sat on.

"The most important thing to do, if we were to restore the building and not pull it down and rebuild, was to conduct a soil test," his voice gathers a sober tone. "We bore sufficient boreholes so that we could extrapolate the profile of the soil foundation. What we found was not pretty, actually the situation was grave. Because of the soft soil, the City Hall was already subsiding. There was a difference of nine inches from one end of the building to the other end. So, in no time, there would be cracks, and it would be difficult for windows and doors to be closed properly as they would be warped. We found that it was very, very poor soil. We only hit hard ground very many metres below the surface at the ground floor level. At that time, there was no basement — basements were expensive to build. And in the early days, there were not so many cars, so there were no car parks."

The result of the soil test and the need for 200 to 300 parking lots made the original estimate by CPG Consultants unrealistic. It was not an option to have no car parks. "We went through several iterations.

We even considered car parks under the Padang. Then we did an estimate for two levels of a basement car park under the two buildings. Two level basements would not take us to the good soil. We needed one more level, three levels to take us to the good soil, and the basement would connect the two buildings."

The bearer of bad news is not a popular guy, but Seow Chuan knew that from the start. He was not in it to be popular or for the fame, it was more important to be right — his reputation was on the line. He saw it as national service, and in this case, pushing forth truths that were tough for his bosses to swallow.

"Because of the amount involved, it had to be a Cabinet decision," he leans back, folds his arms. "I had to be the bad guy, but I stayed focused on being professional. I consulted with a few important people and they told me to be bold and professional. I did not want to lie; I could not compromise, otherwise it would be disastrous later and I would regret not letting them know the truth. They had $40 million put aside as a contingency, and I was asking for a lot more than that. At the presentation to the Cabinet, every important minister was there. Michael Koh, the CEO of Heritage Board then, made the presentation. They all knew he was the spokesperson, and that the architectural team and CPG Consultants were the ones that came up with the final estimates. The case we put forward was straightforward: if you want a good building that fulfils all your criteria of being a world-class institution, then you needed to approve the revised estimate. In many ways, we did not give them any choice, and in the end, the Cabinet accepted."

Municipal Offices, Singapore

The Big Restoration

A steering committee, initially chaired by Dr Balaji Sadasivan, Senior Minister of State for the Ministry of Foreign Affairs and Ministry of Information, Communications and the Arts (MICA), oversaw the art gallery's implementation plan. The steering committee was supported by an Executive Committee and four advisory groups who provided advice on museology, architectural conservation, finance and communications.

"I stayed with the Gallery officially for almost a decade, from 2005 to 2015," he looks up from the book, *The Making of National Gallery Singapore*. "My role as Founding Chairman and Chairman of the Executive Committee for the development of the project was to spearhead the concept, planning and oversee the entire process leading to the successful restoration of the two monuments. In other words, I needed to deliver the buildings ready for the art to be hung when the Gallery opened."

At an Institute of Policy Studies forum, then-Gallery Director, Kwok Kian Chow, noted that "a great museum begins with great public ownership of the institution."[4] Perhaps this sentiment was what propelled the bold choice to hold an international architectural design competition to select the best design and architect for the Gallery.

"It was one of MICA's objectives to explore all possibilities for the best adaptive reuse of the City Hall and the Supreme Court buildings," recalls Seow Chuan. "Organised by MICA, in conjunction with the Singapore Institute of Architects, the international architectural design competition hope was for a wide range of possibilities to emerge, not just from Singapore, but also globally. We basically announced to the

---

[4] IPS, *Making The National Art Gallery of Singapore 'Great'* by Tan Simin and Bhavan Jaipragas.

world that we have this ambitious plan, asking for them to come help us realise it. It was also the hope that besides functioning as a gallery for the visual arts, the new buildings would also redefine their place and space against surrounding areas in the Civic District."

On 23 February 2007, the two-stage architectural design competition was launched. The first stage of the competition called for design and concept proposals, and began on 19 March with a site tour of the two buildings for competing architects to come up with design concepts and ideas. The open design competition drew enthusiastic responses from the local and international community, with a total of 111 entries from 29 countries worldwide, distributed almost equally among the three regions of Europe, North America, and Asia-Pacific, including Singapore. Five proposals were shortlisted in May 2007. Members of the jury consisted of a panel of eminent local and international professionals headed by Tommy Koh, Singapore's Ambassador-at-Large and then-Chairman of the National Heritage Board, and included officials from the URA, Musee National des Arts Asiatiques-Guimet in France and the Asian Civilisations Museum.

As part of the competition package for Stage 1, a detailed design brief was issued, emphasising the need for an appropriate urban response to the history and character of the Civic District while meeting the functional objectives of the Gallery. Pedestrian connectivity, links to public transport and key buildings in the surrounding Civic District were to be addressed as part of the design concept, as they would play a crucial role in drawing visitors to the Gallery.

Another important design consideration was the preservation guidelines drawn up by the Preservation of Monument Board for both buildings. The guidelines required key architectural features of the buildings to be preserved intact, such as the façades, City Hall Chambers and ceremonial front steps of the City Hall, domes, rotunda, courtrooms and Chief Justice's office and chambers.

"The key challenge was that these two buildings were essentially hallmarks of British imperial architecture, where structure, not style, was created to endure," says Seow Chuan, as he flips the pages of *The Making of National Gallery Singapore*. In these two buildings, the serious nature of the business of state, whether administrative or serving the process of justice, was conducted. In contrast to the ostentatious exterior, the interior was rudimentary and functional, not meant to show anything as profound as art. Now, these buildings had to be literally transformed; to be seen as a larger art object in and of themselves whilst protecting their setting and recognising the historical elements that were part of their original makeup. History, culture, art.[5]

For the second stage, the shortlisted candidates had to develop their designs, from which the winning proposal would be selected by the jury. Due to their status as national monuments, certain aspects of the buildings could not be altered, such as the façade of the surrender chamber, the office of Singapore's founding Prime Minister and the panelling in four rooms of the Supreme Court. However, this still left many design options open such as the addition of a roof to connect the two monuments and three basement floors. The participants also had to submit entries within a budget of $320 million.

"To be sure, the entries were judged not just based on how both buildings would serve as galleries," says Seow Chuan, now refreshing himself on the page of the book about the shortlisted entries. "All entries were also judged based on their ability to present a 'big idea' or winning concept for the Gallery. In other words, an entry must demonstrate an

---

5 *The Making of National Gallery Singapore* by Pauline Ang, National Gallery Singapore.

understanding of the opportunities and constraints of the site and the buildings; the historical, urban and social context of the Gallery; and an appreciation of the future role the Gallery would play in the Civic District and in Singapore's cultural landscape."

On 29 August 2007, the seven-member international jury panel named the top three designs out of the five shortlisted. The three firms were Studio Milou Architecture from France, Ho + Hou Architects from Taiwan, and Chan Sau Yan Associates from Singapore — each received $150,000. The jury made their decision after appraising models and digital mock-ups, as well as engaging the five finalists in a presentation and question-and-answer session.[6]

In May 2008, Studio Milou Singapore, in partnership with CPG Consultants (Singapore), was appointed to design and build the Gallery. Studio Milou is a French architectural firm, with branches in Paris and Singapore that specialise in the design of museum and cultural spaces. CPG Consultants has extensive expertise in the conservation and preservation of buildings. By then, they had completed over 20 such projects in Singapore, most of which are gazetted monuments.

Studio Milou Architecture's winning design consisted of a linear draped canopy supported by tree-like columns to link the former Supreme Court Building and City Hall at the roof level. The design incorporated an extended staircase linking the basement to the upper levels. Fine metal mesh was proposed to cover the open area between the Supreme Court and City Hall. Panel members agreed it had "the most delightful design and was well thought through".

On 21 December 2010, Takenaka-Singapore Piling Joint Venture was appointed as the main construction contractor for the new Gallery.

---

[6] Ibid.

The construction works on the buildings began in January 2010 and the National Gallery opened its doors to the public officially on 24 November 2015.

"Construction was supposed to be completed in 2013, and we were supposed to start in 2008. Construction only started in 2010," Seow Chuan remembers with a laugh. "The construction industry was oversubscribed during this time. The government had already decided on the two casinos, so it was tough to get workers and construction materials. The casinos were income-generating, and the Gallery wasn't, so it could wait. They postponed the Gallery. But those two years of postponement was a godsend. The extension gave us time, allowed more breathing space to rework on the tender construction documents. For example, what kind of engineering and architectural details needed to be incorporated into the tender, and how to call for the tender. You see, the building of The Esplanade — Theatres on the Bay had been a huge learning experience."

If the years in DP Architects taught him anything important about a major building project, it was that, one: after a contract was awarded to the contractor, any changes the client made meant a delay of anything from one to 12 months and an increase in cost. And, two, in the end, it was the contractor who would build the project, not the architect or engineer.

"I was very careful, my role as Chairman of the Executive Committee was to make sure that I could justify the estimate we quoted, and, once we got it, to stay on budget. Here, the key was to work with the contractor. No matter how experienced the architect or engineer was, they could not match the experience of the contractor's procuring team," Seow Chuan's voice is now emphatic. "The architect or engineer may specify something but the contractor may have four or five suppliers who could do the work, nearly the same but not with the same brand. So, I learned, the best tenders came from those that use generic terms, not specified terms or products so that you allow the contractor to source most efficiently, economically." He closes the book and looks up at me. "I had to modify the standard specification. It was tough to get the architects and the designers to let the contractors be the ones responsible for the project, it was tough to ask them to be generic, not specific. You see, you need to allow the contractor on the ground to source intelligently, let them have enough room to think on the ground and make good economically sound decisions. I kept telling the team, we are not changing the design, it is the use of materials and construction method, and the contractor needed to be in charge. So, we put these specifications in the tender contract. They source, we approve or disapprove. Of course, it was more work for them. Too bad. That was the best way. More intensive, but more teamwork, not top-down. That's why I spent about 40% of my time on-site fighting some of these battles." He pauses, not sure if he wants to continue talking about this.

What about the Singapore and Southeast Asian art collections? His years of collecting Singapore and Southeast Asian art must have been a big boost to the curators. I notice Seow Chuan has stopped talking completely. When he decides to speak again, it is with reluctance, slowly and selectively.

"As the Founding Chairman of the National Gallery Singapore, I wanted a bit more scholarship and research to our art, and I didn't think the Nanyang art was adequately researched and put forward. I thought so much new work had surfaced, and so much new information had surfaced that needed to be verified and included. Grace Fu, then Minister for Culture, Community and Youth, wrote me a letter to say the art ecosystem was important. There must be a buzz. The whole

ecosystem must be vibrant. That meant not just the Gallery but its involvement with the public, the collectors, the private galleries, auction houses, businesses of art were all important in promoting art, because no one party could promote art alone." He pauses again. "Having an A+ hardware, two neoclassical buildings perfectly repurposed, was just the beginning of creating a good museum. While it had taken a considerable period of time to transform the buildings into the Gallery, everyone knew then that it would take an even longer time for the Gallery to evolve and mature into an important art destination."

"There is one very, very key element about negotiating. And that's to be sure the seller has the title to what he is selling. In any negotiation, you need to have all the knowledge and to be firm and bold."

12

The Art of Negotiation

"Ewer with feline-shaped handle from the Belitung shipwreck, ArtScience Museum, Singapore" is licensed under CC BY-SA 3.0. Photographed by Jack Lee, 2011.

Chapter 12

The Art of Negotiation

Buying 60,000 Pieces of History: The Tang Cargo

1996. A 39-year-old German salvager became fascinated with submerged wrecks when his Indonesian employee started describing the translucent, reef-strewn waters of his native island Belitung, which lies between Borneo and Sumatra. Treasure, he said, lay under the waves. The stories proved irresistible. The Indonesian told his stories so visually and convincingly that the intrigued salvager packed his scuba gear and flew to Indonesia, bringing along his employee. The trip was meant to be a summer holiday of diving adventures, but it changed the salvager's life forever.

1997. The salvager gave up his job and moved to Indonesia, swapping central Germany's grim industrial landscape for white, palm-fringed beaches and the azure blue Java Sea. He lived in a waterfront villa that belonged to a former Indonesian government minister. He read up intensively on the rich maritime history of the region across centuries about the world's major ocean thoroughfares, and which were still infested with pirates. He made friends with fishermen and was charmed by how Indonesian divers used improvised breathing masks fed with air pumped from the surface through garden hoses, instead of gas bottles, to reach the ocean's depths.

One day, he followed a lead provided by his fisherman friends, who had shown him a handful of broken pottery they had gathered during a dive. Donning his black neoprene wetsuit and diving bottle, he plunged 50 feet down to a reef off Belitung. Between 1997 and 1998, he salvaged three wrecks, and the last was that of an Arab dhow named 'Black Rock' or 'Batu Hitam' in Malay, loaded with Tang dynasty ceramics.

"I landed on what looked like an ordinary section of coral reef," he told Germany's *Der Spiegel* magazine. "But it was actually an underwater mound the size of a small hill that was built almost entirely of tens of thousands of pieces of well-preserved ceramic pottery."[1]

The mound turned out to be an undersea treasure trove of such massive historical significance that he was eventually able to name a price of more than US$40 million to international buyers. The treasure was part of a huge cargo of eighth-century porcelain that traders from the Chinese Tang dynasty had put aboard an Arab dhow for export to Malaysia, India and what is now Saudi Arabia. Until this find, archaeologists had assumed that 1,200 years ago, China was a relatively backward country which relied primarily on agriculture to survive. They had little notion that during the Tang dynasty, China had already started to set up maritime trading routes, establishing themselves as the first great sea power, 200 years before the Spanish, Portuguese and British.

The work of salvaging the Belitung wreck, or what is now popularly known as the Tang cargo, started in September 1998 and was not completed until June 1999. The salvager's company, Seabed Explorations based in New Zealand, began the painstaking task of desalting and sifting through the archaeological relics in 2000. The company put a

[1] The Belitung Cargo: Secrets of the Sea, Asian Art Newspaper 28 Feb 2017 https:asianartnewspaper.com.

provisional price tag of US$40 million on the cargo, stipulating that the treasures must be bid for and purchased as a single lot. The cargo consisted of some 60,000 objects, predominantly ceramics produced in China during the Tang dynasty (618–907 CE), and it constituted the largest single collection of Tang dynasty artefacts found. Specifically, the kilns were from Changsha, similar to the 1974 Han tomb excavation findings at Mahuanghui in Changsha, now known throughout the world. Changsha wares are innovative in form, variety and design and are part of a vibrant cultural heritage.[2]

"Wrecks of this age were indeed rare finds," says Seow Chuan. "The wreck demonstrates that the region has been a centre of global trade as early as the ninth century. Singapore lies between two oceans, along a busy sea route running from the Middle East to India, Southeast Asia, and China — what had become popularly known as the Maritime Silk Route after the salvage. This network rivalled the more famous overland Silk Route through Central Asia. And Singapore is situated right in the middle of it all."

Why are we talking about the Tang cargo with Seow Chuan? When I heard about his role in this epic wreck story, I insisted on including it in the book. Here, we are talking about a rather unusual skill that he has been associated with: his skill in negotiation. There is no literature on it; newspaper articles, magazines features and TV programmes focus on Koh Seow Chuan's art collection, stamp collection, the skyscrapers he and his team built. The role of a negotiator has never been touched upon. And here in the Tang cargo salvage, why negotiate? Because Singapore had been keen to own the Tang cargo, and the ministries involved all agreed — Koh Seow Chuan would be the right man for

---

[2] The Belitung Shipwreck | SEAArch Southeast Asian Archaeology https://www.southeastasianarchaelogy.co.

the job, the most effective negotiator to bring home the shipwreck at a good price.

"My education, being a hobbyist, and being multicultural has made me a good negotiator," there is fun and seriousness mixed in his voice. "When you are a stamp collector, when you are an art collector, practically every week you are involved in some kind of negotiation. When you want to buy stamps, the stamp dealer offers you this price, and you negotiate with them. If the price is reasonable, you would feel it is stupid or unreasonable to try to negotiate or bring down the price further. But usually, the seller will want to ask for the best price he can get. And that's fair. The buyer on the other hand will buy at the lowest price he can get. I found out, very early in my life, that I didn't want to waste my time on unsuccessful negotiations. Successful negotiation is when the seller names a price that is high, the buyer says it's high, but not too high. If he can bring it down by 20 or 30%, they may be able to reach a common ground. But when the seller names a price that is too far off, and bringing it down by 30% would still be high, I say forget it. I will tell the seller, I think you need this much more than I do. You should continue to keep it until you can find someone who needs it more than you do. Price is all relative. What's the value to me? It may be something connected to my family, or my profession. And I feel I would like to keep it for a long time. So, I will pay the future price."

I am interested to know how he prepared himself for the Tang cargo negotiation, where tens of millions were involved. How does one prepare for a negotiation?

"One word," he says with resoluteness. "Knowledge." He looks me in the eye. "You must have all the relevant knowledge. When I was a stamp collector, I only bought when I had enough knowledge about the stamps. When you buy a piece of art, you need knowledge of the art. You need to acquire the knowledge first before you talk about the price."

Seow Chuan stands, walks slowly to a side table. He looks down at a thick black folder and turns to me. "All in here," he says. He lifts the folder with both hands and, smiling, walks back towards me. "There is one very, very key element to negotiating. And that's to be sure the seller has the title to what he is selling. If a stamp dealer is trying to sell some fake stamps, or genuine stamps but the postmarks are fake, you'd only know that through knowledge, then you either forget about the item completely, or you tell him that you don't think it is right, and why it is not right. And if you still want to buy it, you buy it for research purposes, because there may be more than one of this fake, not just this one. And that happens with items that have appreciated in price. Those that have not appreciated in price, nobody would waste their time to fake them. And it is applicable to everything — photographs, historical documents, rare antique books or a painting. You need to ask, is it the original original? For example, a painting may be so heavily restored to the point that it is also the restorer's work. The restorer may have done more than 70%, so it is really a painting by two pairs of hands. Also, there are paintings executed by two artists. Or, there may be other similar paintings by the same artist that are in much, much better condition, so why go for something that has been so heavily restored? There are all kinds of details and intricacies, and you can only tell with robust knowledge and experience."

The salvager was German. He was represented by a young German agent who would negotiate on his behalf.

"The salvager and his agent approached then-Minister of Trade and Industry George Yeo," he begins. "George Yeo saw the importance and value of the Tang cargo. So he, in turn, approached the Singapore

Tourism Board. The cargo, George Yeo told them, was important for Singapore to have. He asked them to negotiate with the salvager and his agent." Seow Chuan opens up the black folder. Each document in it has been carefully slotted into place and protected by plastic. He hands me a 12-page report done by an expert. "You don't have to read the whole report now, just the conclusion."

> *The archaeological salvage of the Batu Hitam shipwreck has unlocked the secrets of the sunken ship and greatly expanded our knowledge of the Tang era. It is the oldest ship ever found in Asia, in Indonesian waters, and provides the earliest evidence of the flourishing trade between China and Middle Eastern countries via a maritime silk route. The cargo is of historical importance and can be classed as a world heritage find. The collection is a meaningful and important acquisition for Singapore as Singapore is currently an important commercial and maritime centre in the region. An exhibition of this well-preserved and stunning collection, especially the Changsha wares, at the Singapore Maritime Silk Route Museum would further enhance Singapore's reputation as the gateway to Asia and the link between East and West. More importantly, the collection would help the government to forge closer bonds between Singapore and the Middle Eastern countries. The purchase of the Batu Hitam cargo would enable Singapore to maintain an important cultural heritage in this region. It would also contribute, in no small way, to the revitalization of Singapore's tourism industry and help Singapore to become a world-class destination with its rich offerings of art and cultural products.*[3]

[3] Belitung Shipwreck — Revisit, Changsha Blue and Copper Red Wares and The Religious Motifs www.koh-antique.com.

Three ministries were involved: the Ministry of Trade and Industry, the Ministry of Finance, and the Ministry of Foreign Affairs. But the body fronting the acquisition of the Tang cargo was the Singapore Tourism Board (STB).

"Pamelia Lee of STB approached me," he recalls in a low voice. "I had known her husband for many years. She asked if I was interested in being their chief negotiator. Like everything else, it all starts with knowledge. Since I had the knowledge, I asked myself, was there anyone else in Singapore who could do this better than I could? I needed to be honest with myself, because this was for Singapore. Through my collection of stamps, art, old books, documents and antiquity, I was familiar with what I would be encountering. My family was into antiques, I was familiar with China because of my familial links to China. And in Melbourne, apart from architecture, I attended philosophy and legal classes. I was familiar with contract law. The combination of all these factors gave me the courage to do this and do it well. I began by spending hours combing through the data."

He reminds me, data is the most important. The more data he has, the more he can connect them, and then, the more important every piece of data becomes. But before he started officially, he wanted something else established.

"When I buy something for myself, I am alone," he asserts. "This, I would be doing for the government. And there were other people involved. And usually, for a seller, he will always go to the person with the least resistance to clinch the deal. And I know, in Singapore, when you represent the government, you are more important. If you had to choose between two persons of equal standing, you always go for the government person. It's safer, he has the whole government backing behind him. A private sector person doesn't have that. So, I said, appoint me legally to be chief negotiator." He sits back, and a smile appears. "Thankfully, I asked for it, because I foresaw that I was going to need it, or at some point I would need to call on my legal status."

After reading and learning as much as he possibly could on the contents of the shipwreck, Seow Chuan's next move was to call upon his extensive network of friends from the art world, starting with international auction houses. He quickly learned that Singapore might be the only country truly interested in owning the cargo; the price tag was too high for most of the other relevant countries. Chinese experts had come out to authenticate the salvage, but they also said it was too expensive for them to purchase it. The Indonesians felt they should be paid something of what the salvager was asking, but they showed no interest in owning the cargo. No one in the Middle East showed any real interest either. This became the single most important piece of knowledge for the negotiator going into the negotiation.

Now, Comes the Hard Part

"At the first meeting I had with STB, they told me the agent for the salvager wanted US$48 million," Seow Chuan remembers with a laugh and a slow shake of his head. "We couldn't afford that. I asked STB for the price Singapore would pay, as the official negotiator, the range I could work with. They said between US$24 and US$32 million. So, what I had guessed — 50 to 65% of the asking price. STB also said they needed to figure out where they would find the money for the wreck. They did not want to commit to an amount. They said, you come back to us when you feel there is a chance of closing the deal."

Next, Seow Chuan went to see the cargo himself. The most valuable parts were stored in Bonn, Germany, the rest were kept in New Zealand.

"I must say, seeing the cargo made me excited, and I felt I wanted to do this for Singapore. The wreck predated all accredited Asian discoveries by almost 500 years. There were close to 60,000 pieces, mainly two types, namely tributary wares, which included gold, silver objects and fine porcelain; and trading wares, mainly bowls, some with religious inscriptions and symbols that were Islamic and Buddhist. They had survived remarkably well for 1,200 years, because they had been preserved underwater in mud. The entire hull of the ship was intact. I also felt very good that the cargo had been researched and authenticated by art historians and experts. Now that I had seen the goods, I was ready to talk."

The agent for the salvager was a young negotiator. From his name, Seow Chuan assumed some royal connections back home in Germany. "He had set up an office in Singapore, and would come to the Mandarin Hotel in Marina Square to have drinks with me. I don't know what his commission was, but it must have been worth his while. He spoke well, knew his stuff and was an informed negotiator. The salvager must have had a lot of confidence in him, leaving this young man alone to get the best price for him. I took my time, was always careful to sound interested but not too interested. At the back of my mind, I was always prepared to walk away from it." He pauses, breathes out deeply before he continues. "And so, it went on for two years with the agent. The real bottleneck was his inability to provide me with the title for the goods. The question that hung over the negotiations was the uncertainty of how much claim the Indonesians had over the cargo. I was very sensitive not only about the legality of the purchase, but also the political consequences of such a purchase with Indonesia. So, every step we took with STB and the Ministry of Trade and Industry (MTI), we also alerted the Ministry of Foreign Affairs (MFA). And MFA would check with the Singapore Embassy. We were mindful about the political situation in Indonesia at that time. We did not want a situation where the purchase of a wreck in Indonesian waters became an issue brought up by the political parties in an Indonesian election."

For the law of the sea, Seow Chuan consulted Tommy Koh. "Tommy linked us directly to the Singaporean Ambassador in Indonesia, as the wreck had been salvaged in Indonesian waters," his face shows he is deep in thought. "The conclusions from the two or three discussions with them were that 50% of the ownership was with the salvager and the other 50% was with Indonesia. The salvager did not have the full title. For the Indonesian side, I was also curious, who would represent the country? Which ministry, which department, and how were we going to go about getting clearance? The Singapore Embassy helped to determine the relevant departments. The Embassy contacted them and found out that a sale was indeed possible, that the salvager needed to buy out the rights of the goods from the Indonesians. In other words, the Indonesians were interested in the value, not in the goods."

The salvager had invested considerable cost in carrying out the salvage operations over several years, and had borrowed from banks to fund these costs. At some point, he had to repay the banks. So, he had to name a price for the salvaged wreck whereby he could still make a profit after repaying his loans. That would enable him to share the profit with the Indonesian government.

But the agent stood firm, he represented the seller who salvaged the wreck. The salvager owned it, and the price remained unchanged, at US$48 million.

"I told the agent we were not interested, and called off the negotiations," Seow Chuan leans forward, puts his hands on his knees. "No more negotiations. The agent, of course, tried to persuade me to continue. I told him, you really don't have the title. For the deal to conclude, you need to have full title before we can really negotiate with you and talk about price. So, no title, no offer."

Wen Gin listens quietly, as if she is hearing the story for the first time. She stands suddenly, "Your usual? It's approaching noon."

"Yes," again he shows his appreciation with a wide grin. He turns to me to continue the story. "The agent was adamant. He said STB had already agreed, and he quoted the price of US$48 million again. Then he went further. Through his lawyers he issued a writ of summons to STB."

There is a pregnant pause. He has come to the point in the story that he wants to underline and emphasise. "I told myself, I was lucky I had the chief negotiator legal document. Through Rodyk Davidson, our lawyer, I gave a written affidavit against this writ that the agent's writ had no legal standing. I had informed him that I was the chief negotiator and that here was the legal document appointing me as the chief negotiator, as proof. Anyone could have said he or she agreed with the US$48 million, but they were not the legal negotiators. I was. Rodyk Davidson sent the affidavit to their lawyer, essentially telling the agent that the writ had no substance. The agent then wrote directly to George Yeo, asking me to withdraw my affidavit. George Yeo wrote back to him diplomatically, saying, I know Koh Seow Chuan, and he is an upright man. I am sorry but I cannot do what you ask." He flips the folder to the page that shows the legal correspondence.

Seow Chuan knew no other country was interested in buying the wreck, so he walked away from the negotiation, knowing full well that it was only a matter of time that the salvager would return to the negotiating table and agree to the necessary requirements. In the meantime, he consulted the director of an international auction house, whom the agent might have consulted too. The salvager had made it quite clear he did not want to sell the wreck to any international auction house, as it would invariably be broken up in an auction. He wanted to sell the wreck as one group or collection, with everything intact.

Time was not on the salvager's side; his biggest fear was Singapore losing interest and moving on to something else. For example, when Seow Chuan consulted an official of the Singapore Antiques Association, he was told not to bother with the wreck. Although the salvager told everyone he had the entire wreck intact, all 60,000 pieces, there were reports that there could have been more than 60,000 and also rumours that some bits and pieces of the wreck were selling in the open market for small sums of money. For a while, Seow Chuan did not hear from the agent, then he learned that the agent had stopped working for the salvager.

From the beginning in September 2002, all the way to July 2004, the agent and the salvager held the asking price firm at US$48 million. Then...

"On 2nd August, in the middle of the night, I got a call from Germany. It was the salvager," Seow Chuan takes a sip of his whisky and lets it move down his throat slowly. "The salvager said, I want to be very honest with you, I need to sell as soon as possible. I will take a flight to Singapore and start serious talks with you and your government."

Events developed quickly from this point onwards. The salvager preferred to sell the wreck to Singapore because Singapore would keep the entire cargo intact and was able to pay the agreed price quickly. Two days later, the salvager was in Singapore. In the end, a fair price was paid jointly by Khoo Teck Puat's family and the Sentosa Development Corporation. The entire Tang cargo negotiation started in 2002 and ended over two years later.

"In any negotiation, you need to have all the knowledge and to be firm and bold," he asserts. "It was imperative that the negotiator had full authority and the confidence of the people he was representing. If he did not have the authority and had to refer back at every turn, the sheer bureaucracy would delay and kill the negotiation. STB gave me the authority to walk away from the negotiation when I needed to. In the end, whether there was a competing bid or not, the salvager went with Singapore because he trusted Singapore; he trusted us. He knew we would take good care of the cargo."

In 2011, the treasure was exhibited for the first time at the ArtScience Museum. The exhibition ran from 19 February to 31 July. In April 2015, it was announced that the Asian Civilisations Museum would house the Tang Shipwreck collection. The Tang cargo has found a permanent home, as the Tang Shipwreck, in the Khoo Teck Puat Gallery of the Asian Civilisations Museum. In 2017, co-organised by Asia Society and the Asian Civilisations Museum, some pieces from the shipwreck were exhibited at *Secrets of the Sea: A Tang Shipwreck and Early Trade in Asia,* which took place at the Asia Society and Museum in New York from 7 March to 4 June that year.

"Most men, when they are able to get out of difficult problems in life, attribute the solutions to their own ingenuity. Seow Chuan thinks of God's hands guiding him."

Epilogue

Conversations with God

Epilogue

Conversations with God

Throughout the book, Seow Chuan has talked about God in a way that is personal and intimate. He believes he has had a relatively good life because he has frequent conversations with God. At some of his most critical junctions in life, he has sought counsel from God and, as a result, has been able to see fresh ways out. This has led him to believe that there are some human problems that cannot be solved by humans alone, that humans need divine intervention. Most people, when they are able to solve difficult problems in life, attribute the solutions to their own ingenuity. Seow Chuan thinks of God's hands guiding him. And he believes in the power of prayer. Perhaps what makes Seow Chuan different from other devout Christians or religious persons is his conviction that a religious person also needs to be practical, that his God is a loving and practical God. Above all, and of foremost importance, a person needs to be guided by kindness, and kindness is one virtue all religions agree on. And he believes in Love as the greatest of all virtues. 'Love one another as I have loved you' has guided him all his life. In the end, a religion is a way of life. "Jesus lives in your heart," he says with a voice full of affection.

Here, in this epilogue, Seow Chuan talks about faith from a tender age, his personal relationship with God, how being a man of principle saw him through his vocation, architecture, and how through architecture he could help lift the human spirit of his fellow people. Finally, he touches upon his feelings about how a country, too, needs to be ruled by the laws of right and wrong.

Q: At what point did you become spiritual?

A: It has always been gestating. Being the youngest in a family of eleven, you see a lot happening with your older brothers and sisters, with your parents over the years. There's never a dull moment. There were also moments that were challenging and tense. So, I had a mixed environment. As a young child, going through all this, and being affected by many things, I remember being curious and having many questions, more questions than answers.

When I was young and still swimming, or playing chess, I was also attending church very often. At around 13, 14, and 15, I attended the Sunday school Bible classes. I got baptised at the age of 14. I am Methodist — I attended the Wesley Methodist Church. In ACS, every Friday morning, we had the principal's morning message in school. It was always a passage from one of the gospels of the Bible that he would quote from. I spent six years in ACS, from primary four to secondary four. This combination of school and Sunday school church services, and my parents being Methodist as well (their church in Telok Ayer preached in Chinese), meant I had a strong foundation. But it didn't mean I understood everything or had all my questions answered. And as I got older this foundation got even more mixed. While I did a lot of Bible study, and it gave me a foundation of Christian life, I was also reading very widely, like about the various life forms on earth.

When I was in Melbourne University, the dean allowed me to study philosophy on top of architecture, Western and Eastern philosophy. I also studied the history and philosophy of art and the history and philosophy of science. That combination was useful. It was in university that I started to connect the dots, and saw the connection of things. I became more settled in university because I allowed myself to accept that not everything could be explained scientifically. A lot of things cannot be explained, everything boils down to believing and trusting. And in believing and trusting, my faith in God grew.

Q: Unlike most architects, you speak of architecture almost in spiritual terms. You use terms like, "uplifting the human spirit". How did the world of buildings and the world of God come together for you?

A: Starting an architectural practice, and becoming a partner of Design Partnership and later DP Architects, was intense. I must admit, during those initial periods, the church took a backseat. But I have a bedrock of solid religious grounding to fall back on. Which is why I always say, one's formative years are very important. My formative years saw me diving deep into philosophies both from the East and West, so a sense of right and wrong was deeply ingrained in me. Therefore, even when I had to make business deals where big sums of money were involved, I had a solid ethical compass. This compass gave me a quiet confidence that others could see. After a while and over a few projects, my partners and clients knew who I was, where my centre was. My architectural practice and partnership were all based on good faith, complete integrity and honesty, and passion in doing the work.

Q: You mentioned you believe in the power of prayer.

A: I must say, architecture wasn't a bed of roses. There were many troubling times, the pace was punishing, many days of working late, late into the night. I remember, each time when I was pushed, I went back and called on the foundation of my youth. I believed in the power of prayer. I prayed constantly, regularly, daily. Over a period of time, I found that a lot of my prayers were answered. My faith was strengthened because of the positiveness of prayer. Prayer gave me positive energy, as well as comfort. It was accompanied by making the effort when a direction was indicated. It slowly gathered momentum and I found myself having daily conversations with God, expressing my concerns, my fears when I did not know which direction to turn to. I think on the whole, I have been honest with God, and when my prayers were answered, I grew stronger until it became like a pillar of my DP Architects practice. Up till today, I feel the hands of God blessing the firm, guiding the leaders. Our philosophy from the start was to uplift the human spirit and create a better life for all, and that is still the spirit of DP Architects today.

Q: Design Partnership became DP Architects in 1975. What led to this?

A: In life, you can always talk about problems, lament and criticise, but eventually, let's put all that aside, and ask, what can be done? What is the positive and practical solution? Don't just procrastinate and complain. So, I think I must have prayed. I knew Design Partnership was a partnership. It was not a legal entity. If anyone went, the partnership would be dissolved and would have to be reformed. So, we had one partners meeting when we said, Design Partnership is to be dissolved, the four of us are going to reform a new firm called DP Architects. That was a critical moment for the firm, and I must say, I felt God's hand the entire time. In 1981 a similar problem surfaced. One of the four directors resigned, leaving Chan Sui Him, Gan Eng Oon and me as the directors of DP Architects. And that was the clean start DP Architects had, to grow and be what it is today. I trust God and leave my life in his good hands. On my part, I know he expects nothing but the best of me, so I try my level best.

Q: What is your approach to other faiths?

A: I believe in the Almighty God. All faiths link back to him. I believe it must be so. The Bible says, you are saved by the grace of God through Jesus Christ. What happened to all the people before Christ? Or to those who lived in other parts of the world that are not exposed to the Christian faith? You mean God differentiates? I think there could only be the Almighty God. One that is loving and compassionate. It is human interpretation that draws people apart. Some religions preach exclusivity. If every single faith says that, then, the end of the world would be a war of faiths.

Q: As a Christian, how do you reconcile with some branches of Christianity that say if you are not Christian, you are not saved, and you will go to hell?

A: When I was 14, before I was baptised, I was curious and had a conversation with a preacher. He was a more liberal preacher who shared my own thinking. He offered me a way out. He said, "In this world, everyone is a sinner. Whether you can be saved or not saved is only a concept. It is how you live your life. Everyone is a sinner."

Knowingly or unknowingly, he gave me a very exact phrase. In the Christian church, no one talks about the sin of grace. The idea that one receives the grace of God through Jesus Christ; therefore, one is saved. The belief is that because of that grace, one is saved, and everyone else is not saved if they don't believe. By doing so they are advocating that other than themselves, everyone else is not saved. They are driving fear. They are saying that for you to become Christian, for you to embrace the Christian faith, you have to act that way, otherwise you will go to hell. But do you think our God is that kind of God? Then why create me? Why create me to die and then go to hell? So, I say, everything is based on how you live your life. Regardless of whether you are Christian or not Christian. Throughout history there are many people who have done good things in the name of God, and there are many people who have done bad things, also in the name of God.

Q: Do you feel you have been handed this good life because you have been kind to others?

A: Perhaps. I think kindness is an important element of Christian life. On earth, for a lot of humans, kindness is seen as a weakness. Not a strength. They think, if you are kind, you are not a strong person. If you are kind, you are weak. That is why religion is important. Here is where all religions have a commonality because kindness is priced highly in all religions. For example, Buddhism, which extols the value of kindness, is widespread among the Chinese. Buddhism is also practised in Japan, Korea, the subcontinent of India and other parts of Southeast Asia. Buddhism is not a religion, but a way of life. My belief in Christianity is also my way of life. But the belief must be translated to living it and "doing unto others how you would have them do unto you".

Q: At the national and international level, in secular society, I suppose the rule of law is the 'religion', therefore we must all have faith in the rule of law.

A: It is important for people to have faith, any faith. Religions and related social and cultural structures have played an important part in human history. As mental structures, they influence the way we perceive the world around us and the values we accept or reject. As social structures, they provide a supporting network and a sense of belonging. What is that thing that nags you at night or nudges your mind when you are about to make a decision? Conscience. The Christian faith teaches me that every human has a conscience which has been placed there by God. It is the sense of right and wrong that we all have. The Bible contains God's standard for right and wrong, but even those who have never even heard of the Bible still know the difference. This is because God has placed a sense of right and wrong in their hearts. Actually, you can look at any culture from any time period anywhere in the world and see that human beings have basically the same sense of morality. Almost all cultures forbid murder, stealing, lying and cowardice. This is evidence that God has placed a conscience in all of us. But the Bible also says that it is possible to violate our own conscience so many times that we don't hear it anymore. If we ignore it enough times, we become deaf to our own inner voice. When that happens, we are very far from God. Or we have forsaken God. As the Bible tells us, 'Seek and you shall find. Knock and the door shall be opened unto you. And do unto others what you would others do unto you.'

Q: You are 84, how finished or unfinished is your canvas?

A: Life is like a race, once you start you can't stop. I feel maybe I am at the 75% point. If it is 200 metres, four lengths, I have swum three lengths and I am now turning into the last stretch. And for the last length, you must give all you've got. It's the homerun, you can see the finishing line. The ACS motto is, the best is yet to be. For my last 50 metres, I want it to be a finish guided by God. It may or may not be about me, it could be people who need my help, causes that need my attention or unresolved issues that require my blessings. I like to think I am 84 years young. I may surprise not just others, but myself. Remember, I am an unfinished canvas. I may not want my canvas… finished.